MIND WARS

AVOIDING DECEPTION IN AN AGE OF MANIPULATION

CONNOR BOYACK

LIBERTAS PRESS
SALT LAKE CITY, UT

Libertas Press
2183 W. Main #A102
Lehi, UT 84043

Mind Wars: Avoiding Deception in an Age of Manipulation

ISBN-13 979-8-88688-014-4 (paperback)

For bulk orders, send inquiries to info@libertas.org.

CONTENTS

Other titles by the author:

Children of the Collective

Mediocrity: 40 Ways Government Schools are Failing Today's Students

How to Not Suck at Life: 89 Tips for Teens

Skip College: Launch Your Career Without Debt, Distractions, or a Degree

Lessons from a Lemonade Stand: An Unconventional Guide to Government

Passion-Driven Education: How to Use Your Child's Interests to Ignite a Lifelong Love of Learning

Feardom: How Politicians Exploit Your Emotions and What You Can Do to Stop Them

The Tuttle Twins children's book series

To all those who speak the truth

when it matters most

Propaganda is the executive arm of the
invisible government.

—EDWARD BERNAYS

INTRODUCTION

Wrura, awree? "Brother, do you hear me?" Lieutenant Bradley asked in Pashto, one of the official languages used in Afghanistan. *Mung te ta mrasta be wukawu.* "We're going to help you," he said to the unresponsive young boy lying before him.[1]

Bradley's patient lay on a burlap stretcher, his naked body covered with a brown blanket. Blood was everywhere, and the boy's head was covered in soaked bandages, barely holding his brains in his damaged skull. The wound was still contaminated with rocks and shrapnel. Things weren't looking good. The boy had been seated on a motorcycle just a few yards from where a suicide bomber had detonated an explosive. It was the late 2000s, and war was being waged in big cities and small villages throughout Afghanistan. "He was an errant passer-by, an unfortunate victim of circumstance," Bradley later explained of his young patient. The soldier fought military bureaucracy to provide medical care to the boy but was denied at every turn, given the seriousness of the wounds and the circumstances at the base. A short time later, the boy passed away. Bradley wrote:

> The years leading up to my first deployment were peppered with stories of combat and injury from the survivors I had encountered. Iraq and Afghanistan veterans were all around me from the day I started college ROTC in 2003, and I didn't even deploy until 2009. Until then, the stories were set things... and you didn't doubt the storyteller or see the casualty with your own eyes. Those [victims] died long before the events ever reached you as a cautionary tale. You didn't hear their breath or touch their blood or look at them and know that they were alive, that they might be saved, that they had just this morning been everyday people. They were instead trivialized as sad milestones in the combat narrative. But not this one.[2]

Lieutenant Bradley was one of nearly a million young Americans thrust into combat in the Middle East in the decades following the 9/11 attacks in 2001.[3] An entire generation of kids was sent to fight people they didn't know for reasons they didn't fully understand. The US government was determined to throw bodies and big budgets at this "war on terror." So Bradley and others traveled half a world away to see face-to-face the carnage combat creates.

To be successful in war, highly trained soldiers like Bradley and his peers are obviously needed. In *The Art of War*, Sun Tzu taught to "Ponder and deliberate before you make a move."[4] Careful planning and preparation are needed for any significant effort—and especially in warfare, where there is an enemy that is preparing to harm and kill you at any moment. But what happens when the planning and preparation don't happen?

As Bradley fought to save a young boy's life, several other soldiers publicly revealed how unprepared they were for battle. They pointed out several problems:

- Soldiers were being sent to Afghanistan after only being given a short briefing on Iraq—another country where soldiers were fighting, but different from what they would experience.
- Only 10 percent of the soldiers in their group were able to effectively use the .50 caliber guns they were given.
- Many of the soldiers who would be assigned to drive a heavy Mine Resistant Ambush Protected (MRAP) vehicle did not know how because they had never learned to drive a stick shift.
- Mandatory trainings were being cut down from the required 40 hours to two hour-long Power-Point presentations.

- Soldiers with mental health problems were being sent into combat without appropriate care or
  attention to their needs.[5]

In the words of one soldier, "I would like to believe
that I'm fully prepared to go to war, but that is just not
the case."[6] This unprepared fighter—despite feeling
ill-equipped for the battle he faced—had one massive
advantage over many others. *He at least knew he was
in a war.*

It may seem silly to say, but the first way to lose a
battle is to not even know it's happening. Imagine a
deaf and blind soldier—or someone with a blindfold
and noise-canceling headphones—thrust into a combat
zone. Unable to hear or see what's happening, he might
fail to react to his surroundings until it's too late. He will
inevitably become a casualty in the conflict. He couldn't
possibly defend himself from an enemy he couldn't see
or hear.

Most of us are like that soldier. We, too, are in a war.
You may wake up in a comfortable bed, shop at stores
filled with abundance, go to school or work or hang
out with friends, enjoy a movie, and have a seemingly
peaceful life, but make no mistake—there's a battle being waged every day, and you're in the middle of it. If
you don't want to become a casualty in the conflict, you
need to realize that there is an enemy attacking you.

Physical war is awful, of course, but the greatest threat you face today is the *psychological* war you are in—and your impressionable mind is ground zero for the conflict. The enemy is a host of "consent engineers"—people in power looking to persuade you to adopt their views and support their evil agendas. There is a war for your mind. If you want to win, you have to first realize it's even happening.

It's estimated that around 75 percent of young people are unfit to serve in the military.[7] What would happen if there was a full-blown war? Would we be able to defend ourselves without sufficient soldiers who can handle the physical and mental strain of war? As alarming as that statistic is, the number is surely higher when talking about the mind wars being fought all around us. Without people even understanding the nature of this war and the enemy we face, vast swathes of society are being controlled without having the capacity to resist. They are unfit to fight back, unaware of the tactics used by those who shape the way we think and act. There are too few trained soldiers in this war who are prepared to engage the enemy.

You're on the right track to avoid that fate—this book can be your training manual in the fight against deception. The goal of *Mind Wars* is twofold. First, we're going to discuss what this enemy is—who is a part of it, what its motives are, and how it operates. Second, you'll learn some important things you need to do to adequately defend yourself... and maybe even go on the offense as well. Empowered with this information, you'll be able to inform your family and friends and help ensure that they don't become casualties in a battle they don't even understand. The stakes are high, and the enemy is extremely powerful. But there's a resistance forming, and it needs people like you in order to succeed.

Ready to begin?

KNOW THY ENEMY

I consider *The Matrix* to be one of the most accurate depictions of our modern world. This fictional story tells of a dystopian future in which humans are enslaved by machines—literally harvested for their biological energy, which the machines rely on for fuel. The hordes of humans are plugged into virtual-reality systems, their brains programmed into believing they are living lives of normality and joy. They do not know the true nature of their existence.

Though small in number, there is a band of liberated humans who fight the machines—or, rather, try to avoid them at all costs as a matter of self-preservation. One of these free men, Morpheus, is on a mission to find and liberate Neo from the Matrix. Eventually, Neo is "unplugged" from the system and introduced to reality. But the process is extremely difficult for him to bear since his entire life has been immersed in a virtual world that he thought was real. With his eyes now opened, he struggles to understand what's actually happening.

In one scene, Morpheus takes Neo into a virtual training—a sort of simulated Matrix. Both men walk through a busy intersection of a crowded urban city, which to Neo looks "real." They are surrounded by people, or at least Neo thinks that is what they are. Seeing his bewilderment, Morpheus offers this lesson:

> The Matrix is a system, Neo. That system is our enemy. But when you're inside, you look around, what do you see? Businessmen, teachers, lawyers, carpenters. The very minds of the people we are trying to save... You have to understand, most of these people are not ready to be unplugged. And many of them are so inured, so hopelessly dependent on the system, that they will fight to protect it.[1]

Today's world—your reality—can be compared to the Matrix. We grow up thinking things are a certain way, and we go about our lives based on those assumptions we were taught. But what we don't realize—what some powerful people don't *want* us to realize—is that this fantasy world is not really what is happening. As this book will explain, we have been spoon-fed a series of lies in order to keep us pacified and compliant—like the slumbering, enslaved humans who provided the Matrix machines with the energy they wanted.

Like the Matrix, our enemy relies upon the support of these deceived people. They are unwitting accomplices in pushing the machine's work forward. While horribly misguided, they are not evil people. It is the *system* that is the enemy—not the ignorant individuals who are caught up in its affairs. The duped masses are our potential allies, not our mortal enemies.

But that's the problem, isn't it? As Morpheus explained, these people "are not ready to be unplugged." They are totally dependent on the system, so much so that they "will fight to protect it." Think of it: Here was Morpheus and his ship full of free humans, hoping to free more people from their false world. And yet, their efforts were met with resistance by the very people they were trying to help. That is the power of psychological war. Control the brain, control the body.

There are also some people who control and benefit from the system and support it with eyes wide open to its evil. These people are the enemy. What's worse is that they often think they have noble intentions; they think their supposedly good "ends" justify their evil "means." They often believe that their efforts to control us are for our own good. But as C.S. Lewis warned, "Those who torment us for our own good will torment us without end for they do so with the approval of their own conscience."[2] Many evil people think that they are doing the right thing.

Our enemy—today's Matrix, you might say—has three primary groups of people that we will review in detail: propagandists, politicians, and pundits.

PROPAGANDISTS

Joseph Goebbels was destined to do something important—or so thought his parents, like all good parents do. Born in 1897 in Germany, Goebbels's parents lived modestly and practiced their Roman Catholic faith. They hoped their son would become a Catholic priest, but Goebbels ultimately abandoned the idea after seriously considering it. Instead, he studied literature and history at several universities, ultimately authoring over a dozen books throughout his life. He certainly had a way with words and found work as a tutor and a journalist for the local paper. This was his passion, and one he was eager to use in the service of a cause he believed in.

But what was that cause? Young Goebbels was still figuring it out, reading voraciously. He adopted a pessimistic view of politics along the way, not feeling at home in any of the German political parties.[3] "To practice politics," 26-year-old Goebbels wrote in his diary, "is to enchain the spirit, to know when to speak and when to be silent, to lie for the greater good. My God, what a dreadful business."[4]

Weeks later, events would unfold that would lead Goebbels into a life of lying for what he believed to be the greater good.

In February 1924, Adolf Hitler was put on trial for treason after his failed attempt to seize power several months before. He had organized a group of 600 Nazis to storm a political meeting with the goal of overthrowing the government and establishing the Nazis as the ruling power. This coup failed, and Hitler was sent to prison, where he began writing out his philosophy in what later was published as the book *Mein Kampf*, meaning "My Struggle."

But now it was the trial, and the consequences for this coup had unsurprisingly attracted widespread media coverage, giving Hitler a platform to promote his narrative—his propaganda. Young Goebbels was impressed by what he heard. More than that, he was enthralled! "Hitler is an enthusiastic idealist," he wrote in his diary. "A man who will bring new belief to the Germans. I'm reading his speech, letting myself be carried away by him and up to the stars. The route runs from the brain to the heart."[5] And Goebbels's brain and heart were both affected. "It is impossible to reproduce what [Hitler] said. It must be experienced. He is a genius. The natural, creative instrument of a fate determined by God. I am deeply moved."[6]

Goebbels joined up, becoming member number 8,762 of the Nazi Party. His literary and communication abilities led him to rise in the ranks, from a small newspaper writer to eventually becoming head of the newly created Reich Ministry of Public Enlightenment and Propaganda in 1933, after Hitler had been appointed as chancellor and seized control of the government.

Joseph Goebbels, the head of Nazi Germany's Ministry of Public Enlightenment and Propaganda

Goebbels and his office of propagandists got to work quickly, extending their reach to nearly all aspects of German culture. They influenced films, requiring all members of the industry to join the Reich Film Chamber and produce movies that favored Nazism and carried subliminal messages. They controlled the content of radio stations across the country and outlawed listening to foreign radio stations, threatening the death penalty for those who distributed news from foreign broadcasts. They created the Reich Chamber of Music to coordinate what music would be prohibited or promoted in order to create a culture that would distract people from the terrorism in the streets. They created the

Reich Press Chamber to control who could be a journalist and to shut down opposition newspapers while taking ownership of most papers in the country. By extending their influence throughout culture—especially by promoting low-cost radios to be able to communicate directly with the people on a regular basis—Goebbels and his peers were able to ensure, in the words of one fellow Nazi leader, that "80 million people were deprived of independent thought."[7]

A group of young German boys view Der Stürmer, Die Woche, and other propaganda posters that are posted on a fence in Berlin.

Goebbels had the approval of Adolf Hitler in his efforts, who noted that propaganda's task "is not to make an objective study of the truth, in so far as it favors the enemy, and then set it before the masses with academic fairness; its task is to serve our own right, always and unflinchingly."[8] In other words, if the truth showed that the Nazis were wrong, then the Nazis would reject it and push their own flawed message onto the German people anyway. Truth wasn't important—power was, "always and unflinchingly." The German people, subjected daily to Goebbels' propaganda machine, were basically indoctrinated into this new way of thinking through a "vast network of propaganda machinery" that gave the Nazis "full control over the expression and dissemination of all thought."[9] As one supportive writer pointed out during the war, this massive propaganda effort extended "to all spheres of public life and... also of private life."[10] Control was the goal, and control is what they got.

How did Goebbels do it? Do you think he came up with all of this on his own? Was he such a media mastermind that he could determine how best to manipulate the minds of the masses? As it turns out, he had a manual—a guide to propaganda, you might say. And despite the Nazi position on Jews—considering them subhuman, like vermin—Goebbels was all too willing to implement the ideas he learned from one Austrian-born Jew named Edward Bernays.

The next chapter will delve more into what Bernays taught and what his followers did to create a propaganda machine in the United States. Put simply, he became a self-appointed expert in how to manipulate people into thinking and doing what people in power wanted—whether that was buying a certain product or supporting going to war. Bernays' writings were bold and backed up by powerful psychological arguments, so they were persuasive to those in power who, like Goebbels, wanted to learn ways to effectively manipulate the masses. And this "guide to propaganda" was just what the Nazis needed to shape public opinion. When Bernays learned that his work was being used by the Third Reich to target Jews in "a deliberate, planned campaign," he was "shocked," but understood that the ideas about propaganda that he taught could be used in both helpful and destructive ways. [11]

Propaganda typically has a negative meaning. We often associate it with someone in authority, like a teacher or politician, teaching falsehoods as truth in order to further their agenda. But there are other ways to define it too. For example, Bernays called it the "engineering of consent." [12] He wrote, "The engineering of consent is the very essence of the democratic process, the freedom to persuade and suggest." [13] That sounds pretty simple, right? It's basically people persuading one another, after all. But Bernays himself pointed out that this is not really what happens. In the same essay, he explained that if there are "pressing crises and

decisions," then "leaders must play their part in leading the public through the engineering of consent" to
accomplish their goals.[14] Put simply, propagandists like
Bernays believe that people in power should get others
to give their consent by "engineering" (or shaping) the
outcome—by saying and doing certain things that will
dupe voters into going along. All that mattered were
the "goals and values" of the consent engineers.[15]

When you think about it, it's a freaky term—the *engineering of consent*. It reveals that there are people out
there whose job is to find ways to get you to think how
they want you to think. They are hired by people who
want to influence you to act in certain ways. These
people aren't happy if you make independent decisions
for your life and choose to spend your time and money in ways that matter to you. *They* want to influence
those actions. They want your loyalty and trust. They
want you to think about *them*. They want you to work
toward *their* goals.

As president, Barack Obama appointed a man named
Cass Sunstein to be the head of the Office of Information and Regulatory Affairs. Known as the "regulatory
czar," Sunstein had influence over how government
policies were implemented on a wide range of issues.
But before his time in government, Sunstein wrote a
book called *Nudge* in which he explained how politi-

cians should "cognitively infiltrate" groups that held politically incorrect views in order to then discredit them.[16] In other words, he suggested fighting people who discuss theories about government conspiracy by actually conspiring to "infiltrate" their "chat rooms, online social networks, or even real-space groups"[17] and to plant ideas and messages designed to shift their perception about the government. Literally, he suggested that the government should conspire to fight conspiracy theorists. All of this, in Sunstein's view, would be an effort to "nudge" people in the "right" direction—an effort he considered "legitimate for choice architects to try to influence people's behavior."[18]

Propagandists. Consent engineers. Choice architects. These people believe that they know better than you and that they should manipulate you into supporting their views. But who are they exactly? They are the people in the shadows, behind the scenes, pulling the strings. They are deeply aware of human psychology—how people think and how our brains can be hijacked through emotional manipulation. They are strategic thinkers and master planners. They are not the broadcasters of the message (those are the pundits) or the enforcers of it (those are the politicians). They are, instead, the creators—the architects and engineers that create the system that others build and use. It is through the actions of politicians and the messaging of pundits that the work of propagandists is seen. We'll analyze propaganda in detail in the next chapter. For now, let's spend a moment on the people we love to hate: politicians.

POLITICIANS

An estimated one percent of the world's population are psychopaths[19]—people who repeatedly deceive and lie to others to manipulate them for personal gain. Lots of these people end up in prison, where around 20 percent of inmates rank this way.[20] That's no surprise, since these frequent liars are more likely to be caught and their actions exposed.

But a larger number of people are what's called "almost-psychopaths," operating in a sort of gray area between being normal and being a full-fledged psychopath. Typically, their actions aren't so extreme that they get in trouble too much. In fact, this group can be worse since they often find their way not to prison but instead into positions of power:

> Far from being on the wrong side of the law, almost-psychopaths might be wildly successful, charming and well-liked, as long as you don't wind up on the wrong side of them. Ken Lanning, a retired member of the FBI's Behavioral

Science Unit, calls such people "pillar of the community psychopaths," the politician, doctor or business executive who lies and manipulates others for their own gain.

"If you're trying to run a business or you're in politics, if you're the boss, being a psychopath can really be a positive thing. You can lie, cheat, steal to get what you want," Lanning said.[21]

Read that again: for politicians, *being a psychopath can really be a positive thing.* They lie professionally. They're good at it, and they get away with it. They claim things to be true that are not, and they use their positions of power to make people think they're right. Like President George W. Bush said, "In my line of work you got to keep repeating things over and over and over again for the truth to sink in, to kind of catapult the propaganda."[22]

"Truth is treason in an empire of lies," as former congressman Ron Paul used to say. (He was one of the few truth tellers, which is why he wasn't a "successful" politician.) And in today's mind war, you are surrounded by lies that prop up the empire. Those who share the truth are punished as traitors, like Julian Assange, who was imprisoned for publishing secret documents that embarrassed politicians by showing

how they were lying and supporting the surveillance
of innocent people.[23] Notably, nobody involved in the
surveillance or lies was held accountable. It is the truth
tellers who are traitors in this mind war.

- And the politicians are good at it. George W. Bush,
who was just mentioned? He campaigned on an anti-
war and anti-empire message, leading voters to support him. "If we don't stop extending our troops all
around the world in nation-building missions, then
we're going to have a serious problem coming down
the road. I'm going to prevent that," he assured voters.[24] Then after 9/11, when he and his team saw a
justification to reverse course, he began extending our
troops all around the world in nation-building missions—the precise opposite of what he had promised.
There were lies about "weapons of mass destruction"
used as a reason to convince Americans that the "war
on terror" was necessary. There were lies about the
economy when Bush decided to use taxpayer dollars
to bail out struggling car companies and famously said,
"I've abandoned free market principles to save the free
market system."[25] That's like saying you're trying to
build a home by stealing one.

Bush's father, George H.W. Bush, was no better at
truth-telling. When seeking the Republican nomina-
tion for president in 1988, Bush repeatedly told voters,

"Read my lips: no new taxes!"[26] Then, as president, he signed a law passed by the Democrat-controlled Congress that raised many taxes. The *New York Post* ran this headline: "Read My Lips... I Lied!"[27] And he did. But he, like his son and so many others, was an almost-psychopath who got away with it. The lie worked because it put him in a position of power by deceiving voters. Over and over again, politicians manipulate voters by telling them things that are simply untrue—lulling them with hollow promises they never intend to fulfill. For example:

- When promoting his healthcare reforms, President Barack Obama told voters, "If you like the [health care] plan you have, you can keep it. If you like the doctor you have, you can keep your doctor, too. The only change you'll see are falling costs as our reforms take hold."[28] This was branded as the 2013 Lie of the Year by Politi-Fact,[29] a group of independent fact-checkers that review claims made by politicians. Why? Because almost 10 million people lost their healthcare coverage when Obama's changes were made, and more than 214,000 doctors opted out of the Obamacare programs, causing many patients to lose access to their desired doctor.[30] And the new law didn't result in falling costs—the cost of health care payments went up by about 60 percent in the first four years!

- As the Nazis advanced throughout Europe, President Franklin D. Roosevelt (FDR) told Congress, "Our acts must be guided by one single, hardheaded thought—keeping America out of the war."[31] As France fell and Great Britain was under assault, FDR kept repeating his campaign promise as he sought re-election: "I have said this before, but I shall say it again and again and again: Your boys are not going to be sent into any foreign wars."[32] But the president felt that war was necessary and that American intervention would be needed. The public, however, was not with him; voters did not favor going to war, which is why he made the campaign promises that he did. So he worked in secret to goad the Japanese into attacking America, provoking an action he felt would lead to the desired result: angry Americans demanding a declaration of war against the Axis powers.[33] That attack came on December 7, 1941, at Pearl Harbor in Hawaii. The rest is history.

- As conflict between Russia and Ukraine broke out in 2022, President Joe Biden told members of Congress, "The idea that we're going to send in offensive equipment and have planes and tanks and trains going in [to Ukraine]... that's called World War III."[34] Just over nine months later, Biden announced that the US military would send 31 Abrams M1 main battle tanks to Ukraine in an escalation of support for their fight.

- During the COVID-19 pandemic, many left-leaning governors shut down their states' economies and forced people to remain at home. Despite public pronouncements dictating these restrictive actions to others, many of them hypocritically acted in violation of their own orders. In Michigan, Governor Gretchen Whitmer visited a bar with friends in violation of her state's restrictions and traveled to Florida to visit her father, despite the state discouraging residents from that kind of travel.[35] Virginia Governor Ralph Northam reportedly socialized in close quarters without a mask, despite urging residents of his state to wear masks in similar settings and practice social distancing.[36] California Governor Gavin Newsom dined maskless at a fancy restaurant, violating his own orders.[37] These and countless other executive officials throughout the country publicly claimed a certain set of behaviors was needed while privately acting quite differently.

The lies could go on to fill many books—of presidents, members of Congress, city council members, and countless others, including leaders in other countries, past and present. It's like George Orwell, the famed author of *Animal Farm* and *1984*, once wrote: "Political language is designed to make lies sound truthful and murder respectable, and to give an appearance of solidity to pure wind."[38] Pretty good description, right? In *1984*, Orwell described a totalitarian state ruled by the Party, whose Ministry of Truth building had inscribed in massive letters the following slogans: "War is Peace. Freedom is Slavery. Ignorance is Strength." The politicians in power compelled citizens to live in a state of propaganda-induced fear, warping the language itself into a "newspeak" where words changed meaning. The Ministry of Peace waged war. The Ministry of Love used torture as a means of control. The Ministry of Truth edited history books to change the narrative of the past in a way that served the Party's views.

Almost-psychopathic politicians are the enemy. Their actions are self-serving, and they manipulate language and truth to serve their selfish desires for power and control. They welcome propaganda as a tool to deceive their constituents and collaborate with these "choice architects" to shape the future, as we will explore in the next chapter. Their moral compass—or lack thereof—seems to stem from Niccolò Machiavelli, a fifteenth-century philosopher who advocated lying for political gain. In his popular book, *The Prince*, he justified all kinds of immoral behavior as valid ways to maintain power. Politicians should not keep a promise they made, Machiavelli wrote, "when such observance may be turned against him, and when the reasons that caused him to pledge it exist no longer."[39] In other words, if it's expedient to ignore what you said you should do, then that's fine. "If men were entirely good," he added, "this precept would not hold, but because they are bad" and won't keep their promise, "you too are not bound to observe it with them."[40] More to the point, Machiavelli suggested that those who want to hold power should "know how to do wrong, and to make use of it or not according to necessity."[41] Better to be the ruler than the one being ruled, right?

In a democratic government where citizens can vote their leaders into power, politicians obtain those positions by winning a popularity contest. As one professor said, "Everybody realizes that the system in

Washington is such that if you're pure at heart, you're
not going to get much."[42] Modern Machiavellians por-
tray themselves as saviors and servants but are often
corrupt and conniving charlatans. They deceive the
public into thinking they are someone they are not.
And this description is difficult to detect. A quote often attributed to the Roman orator Cicero makes clear
why politicians are so effective at waging mind wars:

> A nation can survive its fools, and even the
> ambitious. But it cannot survive treason from
> within. An enemy at the gates is less formi-
> dable, for he is known and carries his banner
> openly. But the traitor moves amongst those
> within the gate freely, his sly whispers rustling
> through all the alleys, heard in the very halls of
> government itself.
>
> For the traitor appears not a traitor; he speaks
> in accents familiar to his victims, and he wears
> their face and their arguments, he appeals to
> the baseness that lies deep in the hearts of all
> men. He rots the soul of a nation, he works se-
> cretly and unknown in the night to undermine
> the pillars of the city, he infects the body politic
> so that it can no longer resist. A murderer is less
> to fear.

In reality, the worst people for the job are the ones attracted to being a politician. It is the almost-psychopaths who, unlike full-blown psychopaths, can appear normal, driven, and successful. As J.R.R. Tolkien wrote, "The most improper job of any man... is bossing other men. Not one in a million is fit for it, and least of all those who seek the opportunity."[43] And to succeed in this opportunity, politicians need the group of people we'll next shine a spotlight on: pundits.

PUNDITS

Throughout the 1950s, Phil Graham was the publisher of *The Washington Post*, a large national newspaper. His father-in-law was the newspaper's owner; he had married into the family business. But Graham didn't view his role as a truth teller. Instead, he believed that the media's job was "to mobilize consent for the policies of the government"[44]—in other words, to persuade people to support the state. And because of those views, he became "one of the architects of what became a widespread practice: the use and manipulation of journalists by the CIA."[45]

Graham was one of many in the media who worked with the Central Intelligence Agency to further its goals. They were hired and paid through a program called Operation Mockingbird. The purpose of the program was to manipulate journalists—and through them, their readers, viewers, and listeners—to support viewpoints favorable to the government. Sometimes the stories promoted by the Mockingbird reporters were entirely false—fabrications conjured up in a dim corner of an office at CIA headquarters in Langley, Virginia. Other times, the story was true, but the way it was presented pushed the person reading or listening to see the story from a very specific perspective and come to a very specific conclusion—the conclusion the government had decided best served their purposes.

By 1975, the story began to unravel, and the CIA admitted to Congress that they had, for decades, been actively manipulating the American people by using the mainstream media to direct their thoughts and opinions. They acknowledged that they worked with journalists and other media personalities to distort the truth in order to fit specific agendas. There were no big announcements made to the public about this—most people never even knew that their government had been purposely and actively manipulating them through radio, television, and entertainment for most of their lives. Then Carl Bernstein (who used to work at the *Washington Post*, of all places) wrote an article in *Rolling Stone* in 1977 exposing how the CIA had "secretly bankrolled numerous foreign press services, periodicals, and newspapers—both in English and foreign language—which provided excellent cover for CIA operatives."[46] He found that journalists not only wrote the stories the CIA asked them to and presented them to Americans as fact, but they often had very close relationships with intelligence officers. They willingly shared their notebooks and actively collaborated with them to craft elaborate lies or to put twists on real stories that made them appear entirely different than they actually were. Bernstein also wrote how the CIA was not merely manipulating the foreign press but the domestic press as well, and went as far as to name the networks, publications, and people who had aided the CIA in their efforts. CBS, ABC, NBC, Reuters, *Time*, the *New York Times*, and more were working for the CIA and being compensated very well financially for their troubles.

When Congress published their report on this media influence, the committee wrote that "The CIA currently maintains a network of several hundred foreign individuals around the world who provide intelligence for the CIA and at times attempt to influence opinion through the use of covert propaganda."[47] But highlighting what was happening didn't stop it. For example, Leon Panetta, director of the CIA from 2009 to 2011, later revealed how the agency had influenced media outlets to "change attitudes within the country."[48] The government would do this by paying people in the media "to deliver a specific message."

The point of all of this is to influence the opinions of the masses. While the propagandists operate behind the scenes and the politicians repeat their talking points, the pundits are the cheerleaders in the media who deliver the propagandists' message and who provide the politicians with an opportunity to sing the same tune. True journalists hold powerful people accountable and challenge authority, publishing unflattering truths that expose the bad actions of politicians. But pundits aren't journalists—they are opinion-shapers who use the media to try to influence how people think. And too often, they act in service of the state—not challenging those in power but attacking anyone who does. They repeat the talking points of the propagandists and give softball interviews to politicians. They aren't watchdogs for the public but rather lap dogs for the elite, obediently acting in whatever way they are told to.

At least with Operation Mockingbird, the CIA tried to remain cloaked. They knew at the time that if the public were aware of how much influence the government had on the media, that people would be outraged. But times have changed. What was once covert is now overt. That collusion between pundits and those in power is now openly flaunted. TV media outlets regularly employ former government officials as commentators and even hosts of their own shows[49]: politicians, spies,[50] political advisors, press secretaries, and even war generals. For example, during the war on terror campaigns during the Bush administration, the Pentagon gave special access and information to former military commanders who were now pundits on various TV news shows. In turn, they "echoed administration talking points, sometimes even when they suspected the information was false or inflated. Some analysts acknowledge they suppressed doubts because they feared jeopardizing their access."[51] At least one of these people later became remorseful. Robert Bevelacqua, a retired Green Beret and an analyst for Fox News, recalled, "It was them saying, 'We need to stick our hands up your back and move your mouth for you.'"[52] And when it's not former government officials repeating the talking points, they can simply give them directly to pundits who will read them without being skeptical about what they say. For example, one reporter who covers the military read a statement from the US Department of Defense word for word, which pushed back on claims that the country had been developing bioweapons in Ukraine. After the reporter read the lengthy piece word for word—without challenging any of it—she was

asked by a colleague whether some of it was true. She
pushed back and said it was true. Why? "I have a fact
sheet," she explained matter-of-factly. "That's what I
was just reading from here at the Pentagon."[53]

A pundit's success relies on having an impressionable audience—a viewing public that is likely to believe
their words and change their minds. Perhaps that's getting a little harder these days. A recent poll of Americans found that half of them believe that "national
news organizations intend to mislead, misinform or
persuade the public to adopt a particular point of view
through their reporting."[54] Only 23 percent believed
that journalists act in the public's best interests.[55] And
only seven percent have a high level of trust and confidence in the media.[56] (One wonders why anybody still
trusts the media these days...)

Despite this general level of distrust, many in the
public continue to fall prey to the same pundits spout-
ing lies again and again. It's like we're living in the fable
of the boy who cried wolf, where a young shepherd boy
repeatedly tricked nearby villagers into thinking that a
wolf was attacking his flock of sheep. After multiple
false reports, the wolf actually did attack. But this time,
when the boy called for help, as he had many times
before, the villagers did not respond. You and I are in a
mind war today where pundits are like the boy, crying

wolf over and over again—claiming things to be true that are false. We have to navigate through the foggy terrain of pundits' opinions to find the truth. It's like Leo Tolstoy said: "The truth is obtained like gold: not by letting it grow bigger, but by washing off from it everything that isn't gold."[57] In our day, this means first recognizing that corporate media outlets have been heavily compromised—whether from covert influence by the CIA and other government agencies or because of collusion in open view of the public, like when government officials are hired to become pundits for the national media outlets. Some journalists have sounded this warning for years. "We lie about everything—lying has become the staple," said investigative journalist Seymour Hersh, who suggested that journalism could be fixed by closing down the main media outlets and firing 90 percent of editors.[58] "Our house is on fire... We're getting the big stories wrong, over and over again," admitted the managing editor at CBS.[59]

But it's not just that pundits openly promote lies and half-truths. What's worse is their unwillingness to push back on the propagandists and hold politicians accountable. Journalism should be an effort to challenge the powerful by investigating their claims. Instead, today's pundits are perversely rewarded for their lies. As investigative reporter Glenn Greenwald wrote, "The journalists who lie most frequently, casually, and aggressively on behalf of government and economic power centers, are the ones who shoot at the top of the corporate journalism ladder."[60] Up-and-coming pundits see that the path to success requires them to play nice with those in power, so they comply. They don't bite the hand that offers to feed them.

Consider this question: Do pundits want their viewers to be critical thinkers and understand the truth? Is that their primary motive? Is that how they make more money and get promoted? To answer this, you have to realize that media companies survive on revenue from advertisers—so the more people who watch a show or read an article, the more money these media companies can earn. They succeed when they get people hooked on their programming. That means they do better with ignorant people who grow dependent upon pundits to help provide them with information and ideas so they can appear informed. Just as a drug dealer wants his clients to become addicts to keep them coming back for more, pundits want their audience to rely on them. This creates a society that has the appearance of being informed while actually being ignorant—full of talking points but lacking truth.

In early February 1981, Ronald Reagan had just begun his first term as president of the United States.

He assembled his cabinet of secretaries, each of whom would oversee various parts of the government. William Casey was the newly installed director of the CIA, with only a few days on the job. In a meeting together, Casey shared with President Reagan some details about the work the agency of spies was involved in. Then he said, "We'll know our disinformation program is complete when everything the American public believes is false."[61] Whether it's Operation Mockingbird or another program the government is involved in today, pundits are useful puppets for those in power to spread their falsehoods as truth. Perhaps this is why Thomas Jefferson once said, "The man who never looks into a newspaper is better informed than he who reads them; inasmuch as he who knows nothing is nearer to truth than he whose mind is filled with falsehoods and errors."[62] Today that applies to TV, radio, podcasts, social media, and more.

Pundits do not want what's best for you. They don't ultimately care about the truth—they want to advance their agenda. They want to persuade you to agree with them. They want to build an audience of loyal listeners, including you. They are the enemy, alongside the propagandists and politicians, who desire power over you and who manipulate you to accomplish it.

PROPAGANDA IS POWER

On May 6, 1856, young Sigmund was born to Jacob and Amalia Freud in what is now the Czech Republic. When Sigmund was four, Jacob, a wool merchant, moved his family to Austria in search of new business opportunities. In this new country, Sigmund later entered the university at age seventeen to study medicine. His research led him to study the brain and how it operates. He eventually stopped experimenting with actual brains and instead tried to understand how they operate—what desires and impulses influence our behavior without our conscious awareness. He studied the unconscious mind and the ways that people can gain greater control over their lives by understanding how their mind operates.

This new field of research, called psychoanalysis, became very popular and led many people to understand the human mind differently. Freud had many adherents, one of whom was his nephew, Edward Bernays,[1] who had moved to the United States. Bernays became a journalist and press agent, promoting various ballets and plays using creative marketing techniques. As World War I broke out, he was hired by the Committee on Public Information (CPI), a government agency created to influence the public's opinion in support of the war. Bernays referred to this work as "psychological warfare."[2] As the war ended, he realized that the skills he had gained in promoting propaganda to the public to encourage their political support of the war could be used for other things as well:

> There was one basic lesson I learned in the CPI—that efforts comparable to those applied by the CPI to affect the attitudes of the enemy, of neutrals, and people of this country could be applied with equal facility to peacetime pursuits. In other words, what could be done for a nation at war could be done for organizations and people in a nation at peace.[3]

Where Freud's work focused on helping patients gain control of themselves by understanding their own mind, Bernays used his uncle's ideas in order to help the government, and then private companies, control *others' minds*. Where Freud pioneered psychoanalysis, Bernays pioneered propaganda and public relations— influencing others' minds to get them to act in a way you want. For example, one of Bernays's early clients

was Beech-Nut Packing Company, the country's largest bacon producer at the time. Throughout the nine-
teenth century, when more workers had to do manual
labor, it was common to eat a large breakfast, including
bacon and eggs, doughnuts, pie, and coffee. But as more
people started working in jobs that required less manual labor, and with more people paying attention to their
weight, the common breakfast had been reduced to
things like toast and orange juice.[4] Beech-Nut needed
to make bacon popular again. So Bernays found some
doctors who were willing to say that a heavy breakfast
was "scientifically desirable," and within months of
publicizing their opinions, bacon sales boomed.

This was child's play compared to what Bernays
would later do. And it was his experience in altering
people's opinions and actions that led him to write
four books explaining how he was able to change people's minds. In *Crystallizing Public Opinion*, published
in 1923, he began defining what "public relations"
means and how a person who works in this field can
get media attention "in order to appeal to the instincts
and fundamental emotions of the public."[5] Five years
later, he wrote *Propaganda*, a revealing book that details how people like him are able to shift the opinions
and actions of the masses without their awareness or
consent. He argued that manipulating people "is an im-

portant element in democratic society" and that those who do the manipulating "constitute an invisible government which is the true ruling power of our country."[6] He continued:

> We are governed, our minds are molded, our tastes formed, our ideas suggested, largely by men we have never heard of... In almost every act of our daily lives, whether... in our social conduct or our ethical thinking, we are dominated by the relatively small number of persons... who understand the mental processes and social patterns of the masses. It is they who pull the wires which control the public mind.[7]

This isn't something that only happened a century ago, when Bernays first wrote about it. This is the very mind war we're in—it's happening all around you today. For example, after Joe Biden defeated Donald Trump in the 2020 presidential race, a group of political insiders wanted to publicly brag about their role in the results while remaining anonymous. *Time* magazine published an article after interviewing these individuals titled "The Secret History of the Shadow Campaign That Saved the 2020 Election." The article says that these conspirators wanted their actions made public "even though it sounds like a paranoid fever dream—a well-funded cabal of powerful people, ranging across industries and ideologies, working together behind the scenes to influence perceptions, change rules and laws, steer media coverage and control the flow of information."[8] This "cabal" is an example of the "men we have never heard of" that Bernays mentioned—an "invisible government which is the *true* ruling power of our country."

This is the power of propaganda—the ability to "engineer" consent.[9] What other examples might exist? What else does this "cabal" work on? Who are the conspirators today manipulating public opinion without people even being aware? In order to defend ourselves in the mind war, we need to understand what the enemy's weapons are and how they are used. Propaganda is the chief method of the enemy's power, and it comes in several forms. Let's review a few of them.

FALSE FLAGS

Nayirah was a young woman from Kuwait who, in 1990, appeared before the Congressional Human Rights Caucus to testify about crimes she had witnessed being committed by Iraqi soldiers. The American military was on high alert after Saddam Hussein sent Iraqi soldiers into neighboring Kuwait. But voters weren't that interested in intervening in the internal affairs of these countries in the Middle East. That is, until Nayirah shared her story.

Through tears, the young girl claimed that soldiers took babies out of incubators in a Kuwaiti hospital and left them to die. One of the congressmen remarked that he had never heard such "brutality and inhumanity and sadism."[10] Many senators cited Nayirah's testimony in their speeches supporting military intervention against Iraq, and President George H. W. Bush repeated the story several times in the following weeks. The news media widely publicized portions of her testimony. To say that Americans were shocked and outraged would be an understatement—the allegations made in the testimony were, after all, quite alarming.

They were also false.

Only later was it discovered that Nayirah was the daughter of the Kuwaiti ambassador to the United States and that she had been coached by an advertising agency that was paid millions of dollars by Citizens for a Free Kuwait—a public relations committee created by officials at the Kuwaiti embassy. As one reporter wrote, "The incubator story seriously distorted the American debate about whether to support military action."[11] But that was the point: Hill & Knowlton, the advertising agency coaching Nayirah and others, had spent a million dollars provided by the Kuwaiti royal family to determine how best to sway American public opinion.[12]

Nayirah Al-Sabah testifies before the United States
Congressional Human Rights Caucus on October 10, 1990

This type of propaganda is called a "false flag," originating from the sea when pirates would falsely fly the flag of another ship's mother country to deceive them into coming close, so they could then launch their attack and take the ship's resources. In today's mind war, it appears in stories like Nayirah's, where the public is deceived into thinking something happened a certain way to stir up their anger and encourage them to support war. False flags are fairly common, as they are an effective way to manipulate the feelings and opinions of the public. Recall the example shared earlier of President Franklin D. Roosevelt, where he goaded the Japanese into attacking America at Pearl Harbor in order to make Americans angry and lead them to demand a declaration of war. Some other notable examples include:

- **Operation Northwoods.** Amid tensions with Cuba's alliance with the Soviet Union, the Joint Chiefs of Staff—the nation's top military officials—proposed a plan calling for the CIA to commit acts of terrorism within the United States to be blamed on Cuba. "The desired resultant from the execution of this plan," the proposal read, "would be to place the United States in the apparent position of suffering defensible grievances from a rash and irresponsible government of Cuba and to develop an international image of a Cuban threat to peace in the Western Hemisphere."[13] It recommended creating a "Communist Cuban terror campaign in the Miami area, in other Florida cities and even in Washington"—a campaign that included hijacking airplanes, blowing up a US ship in Guantanamo Bay, bombing American cities, and sinking boatloads of Cuban refugees desperately seeking a better life. All of this was proposed because "it would seem desirable to use legitimate provocation as the basis for US military intervention in Cuba"; therefore, a "cover and deception plan" was seen as beneficial.[14] In other words, government officials wanted to create public support for aggressive and unprovoked military interventions in Cuba but knew that it likely wouldn't happen without a false flag to scare Americans into supporting their plan. President John F. Kennedy rejected the plan.

• **Gulf of Tonkin.** Communists controlled North Vietnam, while the United States military supported South Vietnam and its efforts to fight its northern neighbors. American soldiers became heavily involved in the conflict in the early 1960s, though a poll conducted in May 1964 found that despite this level of intervention and despite "news of Vietnam [being] headlined in newspapers and on television and radio almost every day," fully two-thirds of Americans "said they paid little or no attention to developments in South Vietnam."[15] This ignorance and apathy were washed away three months later, when a sea battle occurred on August 2 between a US destroyer and North Vietnamese torpedo boats in the Gulf of Tonkin off the Vietnamese coast. Two days later, the National Security Agency (NSA) falsely claimed that another battle had occurred.[16] The captain of a US naval destroyer had sent in a report that he was being surrounded and fired on by enemy boats, but later admitted that he wasn't actually sure because of bad weather and low visibility. Declassified documents released in 2005 suggest that the North Vietnamese navy was not attacking but simply trying to salvage two of the boats that had been damaged in the initial conflict. But President Lyndon B. Johnson ran with the NSA's claims and persuaded the American public, and Congress, to authorize him to start bombing raids on North Vietnam and significantly escalate America's involvement in the Vietnam conflict. Convinced that America's military was being repeatedly attacked, most voters backed going to war[17]—a war that would claim nearly 60,000 American lives and more than three million Vietnamese lives.

- **The Gleiwitz incident.** Reinhard Heydrich was a high-ranking German police official during the Nazi era and later became the architect of the Holocaust. Under his command, German police officers dressed in Polish uniforms on August 31, 1939, and seized the Gleiwitz radio station in Germany, near the border with Poland. They broadcast a short anti-German message and executed a German farmer thought to be sympathetic to Poland. They then dressed him to look like a saboteur and left his body at the scene, so that he appeared to have been killed while attacking the station. His corpse was used as "evidence" of the crime and "proof" for the public to see what happened. The following day, Germany invaded Poland, which led to World War II in Europe. A week prior to the false flag incident, Adolf Hitler had told his generals, "I will provide a propagandistic *casus belli* [an action used to justify war, like a false flag attack]. Its credibility doesn't matter. The victor will not be asked whether he told the truth."[18]

Time and time again, people are deceived into supporting military action or increased government power as a result of false flag propaganda. Military leaders and government officials operate behind the scenes to pull strings and orchestrate events that dupe the public into advocating for war. For example, former National Security Adviser John Bolton publicly admitted in July 2022 to having "helped plan *coup d'état*,"[19] or the overthrow of the government, in other countries. This back-room manipulation of events on the ground is common, yet it always involves propaganda to trick the public into thinking things happened a certain way instead of telling them the truth.

MEDIA INFLUENCE

As war broke out in Europe in late 1914, America stayed neutral. President Woodrow Wilson defended this neutrality, as most American parents didn't want to send their children to fight and die in faraway lands. So when Wilson sought reelection in 1916 and had a tough challenger, his supporters emphasized how Wilson had preserved peace in America. "He kept us out of war!" was the campaign slogan they chanted. Wilson narrowly won.

Just a few months later, the man who had kept America out of war pushed the country directly into it. On April 2, 1917, Wilson asked Congress for a declaration of war against Germany as part of an effort to "make the world safe for democracy."[20] Four days later, Congress approved the declaration, and America's involvement in what we now call World War I officially began.

But there was another war that was launched around the same time, and one that few people talk about. Just one week after Congress declared physical war, Wilson issued an executive order creating a new agency in the federal government that would conduct psychological war—not against Germans but against American citizens. This was the Committee on Public Information (CPI)—the agency where Bernays was employed—and its agents were tasked with shaping press coverage and manipulating public support in favor of the war. Because the country had no standing army at the time, a draft was imposed, and the CPI sold enlistment in the military as a moral obligation. Each of the over twenty bureaus and divisions within the CPI sought to influence the media in order to change the public's feelings about the war. Here are some examples:

- **Division of Four Minute Men.** The CPI recruited 75,000 specialists who became known as "Four Minute Men" since they could sell the war in short speeches that were played during the four minutes it took for the film reels to be changed in movie theaters.[21] Topics were assigned by CPI agents, and between 1917 and 1918, the Four Minute Men delivered over 750,000 speeches in 5,200 communities, reaching about 400 million listeners.[22]

- **Division of Films.** The CPI created newsreels such as the weekly "Official War Review," providing detailed imagery and examples of how ships were built, how soldiers were trained, and how weapons were manufactured and transported—all to generate "arousing enthusiasm" in support of the war effort and to "stimulate the public will to win the war,"[23] in the words of the division's production manager. "Few people realize the tremendous propagandizing force," he wrote, "of the motion-picture news reel—chiefly because its influence is exerted so casually and so continuously..."[24]

- **Division of News.** Among other activities, the CPI produced a daily newspaper called the *Official Bulletin*, which grew to become a 32-page publication distributed to elected officials, post offices, military bases, news agencies, and more. Its focus was to popularize positive stories about American involvement in the war because CPI leaders felt that "public support is a matter of public understanding."[25] For example, though conditions for US troops preparing to face the Germans were often poor, the CPI portrayed them as well-equipped and ready for the fight.

- **Division of Pictorial Publicity.** Popular artists across America were tasked with producing propaganda imagery to be used on posters, cards, buttons, and cartoons. Overall, 318 artists created over 1,400 designs to support the war.[26] The head of the CPI, George Creel, later wrote that "In some respects [these artists] were the most remarkable of the many forces called into being by the CPI. America had more posters than any other belligerent and what is more to the point, they were the best."

This pervasive media influence to spread the government's desired propaganda was extremely impactful and quite innovative for the time. A 1940 report by the Council on Foreign Relations—an organization that generally supports America's repeated involvement in military conflicts—approvingly noted the influence the CPI had:

U.S. Army Recruitment Poster, one of 46 designs created by artist James Flagg for the CPI's Division of Pictorial Publicity.

In November 1916, the slogan of Wilson's supporters, "He Kept Us Out Of War," played an important part in winning the election. At that time a large part of the country was apathetic.... Yet, within a very short period after America had joined the belligerents, the nation appeared to be enthusiastically and overwhelmingly convinced of the justice of the cause of the Allies, and unanimously determined to help them win. The revolutionary change is only partly explainable by a sudden explosion of latent anti-German sentiment detonated by the declaration of war. Far more significance is to be attributed to the work of the group of zealous amateur propagandists, organized under Mr. George Creel in the Committee on Public Information. With his associates he planned and carried out what was perhaps the most effective job of large-scale war propaganda which the world had ever witnessed.[27]

Let's pause and consider a question: Do you think this method of media influence to spread propaganda ceased to exist over a century ago, or that it is only used in support of a declared war? The very idea is laughable—if anything, the tactics employed by propagandists, politicians, and pundits have grown more subtle and sophisticated, aided by widespread adoption of technology and the proliferation of smartphones and social media. Just a few decades later, the Central Intelligence Agency (CIA) launched Operation Mockingbird to manipulate news organizations and ensure the government's talking points were taught as truth to the deceived, ignorant public. More recently, Elon Musk exposed the collaboration of social media giants and government officials when he purchased Twitter and shared the company's emails and documents with reporters, who found that the "news media became an arm of a state-sponsored thought-policing system."[28] Dozens of former CIA, FBI, and other government agents now work at these large social media companies, continuing to exert influence to shape a particular narrative.

For another example, look at climate change—a topic that those in power love to push because addressing the issue requires more government, more taxes, and more political control. So it's no surprise that the United Nations has strong feelings on the matter. But instead of sharing their views in a competitive marketplace of ideas, they want to change the rules of the game by manipulating what you learn while you search. The UN's Under-Secretary-General for Global Communications announced in April 2022 that when people search for "climate change" on Google, they will find "authoritative information from the United Nations."[29]

> We are happy to team with Google to ensure that factual, trustworthy content about climate

is available to as wide a global audience as possible. Misinformation is so widespread these days that it threatens progress and understanding on many critical issues, including climate. The need for accurate, science-based information on a subject like climate change has therefore never been greater.[30]

The problem here? What politicians call "factual, trustworthy content" is often utter garbage and flat out wrong—and what they call "misinformation" is often true but in conflict with their plans and desires. During the COVID-19 fiasco, when politicians and their friends at Pfizer were promoting vaccines as "safe and effective," they worked with their media allies to smear anyone using things like Ivermectin to treat their condition instead. When popular podcaster Joe Rogan said he was using the drug, pundits swiftly attacked him for taking "horse dewormer" that was "discouraged by the government."[31] Another example is when the Virality Project at Stanford University—which partnered with many government agencies—urged social media companies to delete "stories of true vaccine side effects" and "true posts which could fuel [vaccine] hesitancy."[32] To them, these inconvenient truths were harmful to the narrative they were trying to create—it undermined their mind war to propagandize the public into believing that the vaccine was safe, effective, and necessary to protect their health. Those who refused were told by the government that they would face a "winter of severe illness and death... for themselves, their families and the hospitals they'll soon overwhelm."[33] Of course, none of this was true, but the psychological war had done its damage. Countless millions lined up to do what they were told, their minds manipulated by the media's influence over them.

GROUPTHINK

Media influence helps change an individual's mind, but the collective effect is just as problematic. Let's continue with the COVID-19 situation to illustrate another method of propaganda to influence others: groupthink.

This previously unknown virus began spreading quickly, and billions of people began to fear its potential. Social media fanned the flames of fear, and people panicked. The media put death counts on the screen— the total number of cases and deaths—without any context. Medical professionals counted as a "COVID-19 death" anyone who died for any reason (such as a heart attack or car accident, for example) if they had the virus at the time of death. We were told to act against a common threat and were given opportunities to signal our virtue: first wearing a mask "to do our part," and then getting a vaccine for the same. Just as in an actual war, when critics are painted as traitors, this psychological war encouraged the obedient group to consider its critics as traitors too. Those refusing to wear a mask or get vaccinated were ostracized, punished, fired from their jobs, excluded from family events, and more.

Consider the masks first. On February 29, 2020, the US Surgeon General warned Americans that wearing a face mask would not stop a person from contracting the virus. "Seriously people—STOP BUYING MASKS!" he tweeted. "They are NOT effective in preventing general public from catching #Coronavirus..."[34] The Centers for Disease Control and Prevention (CDC) sang the same tune, saying that healthy people don't need to wear masks. But this soon changed, and suddenly government agencies began requiring individuals to wear one to "slow the spread"—and media outlets in unison began repeating this new social standard and shaming those who didn't comply. This new expectation, set by those in power, became a weapon to badger people into compliance. Teachers, flight attendants, police officers, and even religious leaders all became enforcement officials—along with nosy neighbors soon branded as "Karens"—bringing people into line by making sure the mask covered both their mouth and nose.

And after all of this coercion and conformity, the most comprehensive study on the issue, published in January 2023, found that there was *no evidence* that wearing masks even made any difference.[35]

Or consider the vaccine. SARS-CoV-2, the virus that causes COVID-19, was first identified in December 2019. Just one year later, the Pfizer vaccine became the first to get an "Emergency Use Authorization" from the Food and Drug Administration. The next fastest vaccine to be produced was the mumps vaccine, which took four years. Most vaccines take much longer and undergo significant research and testing, unlike what happened with the COVID-19 vaccine. Despite this rushed result, the vaccine was declared "safe and effective" by politicians and pundits—without any long-term studies to validate this claim. Billions of people lined up to inject their bodies with a newly concocted lab creation, trusting in the near unanimous position of those in power. And then, like with masks, they turned into peer enforcement officers, yelling at the unvaccinated for having the audacity to potentially kill their grandmother.[36] But this groupthink soon destabilized as the "safe and effective" claim began to weaken as more data came to light. Consider this timeline of news article headlines, for this example focusing only on Pfizer's vaccine and only on the efficacy aspect:

- 03/31/2021: The Pfizer Vaccine Is 100 Percent Effective for People This Age, Study Says[37]

- 03/31/2021: Pfizer/BioNTech says its Covid-19 vaccine is 100% effective[38]

- 05/06/2021: Pfizer vaccine 96.7% effective at preventing COVID deaths, Israeli data shows[39]

- 07/22/2021: Study: Pfizer vaccine 88 percent effective against delta variant[40]

- 7/22/21: Health Ministry says COVID vaccine is only 40% effective at halting transmission[41]

- 8/12/21: Moderna Covid vaccine 76% effective against Delta, Pfizer 42%: Study[42]

- 10/7/21: Pfizer's Covid vaccine efficacy against infection plunges to just 20% after six months...[43]

At first, we were told that the "safe and effective" vaccines would stop transmission of the disease—in other words, if you had the vaccine, then you couldn't catch COVID-19. Most people believed it since it's what the authorities told them to believe; this is the power of groupthink. President Biden reassured Americans that "If you're vaccinated, you're not going to be hospitalized, you're not going to be in the IC unit, and you're not going to die."[44] CDC director Rochelle

Walensky argued that "Vaccinated people do not carry the virus [and] don't get sick."[45] MSNBC pundit Rachel Maddow said, "Now we know that the vaccines work well enough—that the virus stops with every vaccinated person."[46] And all the politicians and pundits were backed up by science "experts," such as Dr. Monica Gandhi, an infectious disease researcher, who told TV viewers during her interview that "Essentially, the vaccines block you from getting and giving the virus."

But none of this was accurate, and as the data proved these politicians and pundits wrong—and as the "Big Pharma" propaganda started to break down—the public was swept along with every new position. First, masks were not needed; then, they were absolutely needed. First, vaccines were safe and effective; then, they had safety issues and plummeting rates of effectiveness. First, they were meant to stop transmission of COVID-19; then, suddenly they were *never* intended to stop transmission. The public was led from one position to the next and never apologized to or informed about past mistakes. Those past problems were all swept under the rug, like in George Orwell's *1984*, when Winston Smith, who worked at the Ministry of Truth, was required to send papers and evidence down a small chute that led to an incinerator when Big Brother wanted something censored.

It certainly didn't only happen during COVID-19,
though that is certainly a remarkable example. It happens with war propaganda, climate change, tax policy,
educational mediocrity, and countless more issues.
Consider another recent example: inflation. Here's a
series of headlines showing the changing narrative and
what people were pushed to collectively believe and
accept:

- 4/28/21: Federal Reserve calls inflation
  "transitory"[47]

- 6/10/21: Inflation is hotter than expected, but
  it looks temporary[48]

- 9/23/21: Fed Officials See 'Transitory' Inflation Lasting Quite a While[49]

- 7/13/22: U.S. inflation at 9.1 percent, a record
  high[50]

- 10/19/22: Why inflation refuses to go away[51]

- 4/26/23: People need to accept they are
  poorer[52]

Groupthink basically centers on the idea that individuals are smart, but groups of individuals can be really stupid. We are social creatures, and oftentimes, rather than investigating things on our own—as we would
if we were alone to figure something out—we look to

others around us for cues on how to behave. Irving Janis, the social psychologist who gave this phenomenon its name, suggested several aspects of groupthink:

1. **An illusion of invulnerability:** group members feel overly optimistic about their views and engage in riskier behavior as a result.

2. **Collective rationalization:** when the group adopts a position, its members feel no need to think rationally on their own.

3. **Belief in superior morality:** refusing to question basic beliefs or premises causes group members to ignore moral problems and negative consequences of their position.

4. **Stereotyped views of others:** those not in the group are viewed as enemies, and their views are always cast in the most negative light, or altogether ignored.

5. **Internal pressure on dissenters:** to keep the group cohesive, its members will attack anyone who dissents and refuses to toe the line.

6. **Self-censorship:** group members will censor their own conflicting or disapproved thoughts to avoid conflicts and disagreements with others.

Groupthink is powerful because of the willingness of the majority to attack the dissenting minority, categorizing their (often correct) views as "misinformation." This propaganda tactic is readily apparent in today's society. Consider the words of President Biden's press secretary, Karine Jean-Pierre: "When you are not with where a majority of Americans are, then, you know, that is extreme. That is an extreme way of thinking."[53] If you're not in the group, you're an outcast to be attacked. Groupthink like this is a powerful tool in the mind war that shames truth tellers into silence so the elite can get their way.

...AND MORE

Dehumanize the Enemy

Before soldiers are sent onto the battlefield, they must first be conditioned to view their fellow humans as the enemy—subhuman entities that they should be willing to harm or even kill. As one psychology professor noted, "For most human beings, it takes an awful lot to allow them to kill another human being. The only way to do it is to justify the killing, to make the enemy look as evil as possible."[54] This has happened in every major war. One American stationed in Iraq said of his fellow soldiers, "A lot of guys really supported the whole concept that if they don't speak English and they have darker skin, they're not as human as us, so we can do what we want."[55] An army chief of staff compared Fallujah to "a huge rat's nest" that was "festering" and needed to be "dealt with."[56] In World War I, Germans were depicted as a crazy gorilla with a bloody club; Americans were encouraged to "destroy this mad brute." Germans ordered to kill Jews were first conditioned to believe they were subhuman vermin to be dealt with like diseased rodents.

And this doesn't just happen prior to physical warfare. Long before the Nazi regime, European empires colonized and enslaved other groups, whom they dehumanized as infantile savages. In America, Chinese immigrants were ruthlessly attacked in the mid-1800s because they were seen as an economic threat to locals. Cartoonists depicted the Chinese as strange rat eaters and job stealers, building political pressure that led San Francisco officials to pass a law forbidding people from walking on sidewalks with a pole and baskets over their shoulders (a common practice among the Chinese). Using propaganda, those in power demonize an enemy to dehumanize him, thus making it easier to rally others to fight him.

Consider the climate of fear and anger that seized the United States after the 9/11 attack—an emotional state ripe for waging a mind war. As the government prepared for war in the Middle East, those who dared to voice their opposition to the conflict were smeared by politicians and pundits alike as traitors, unpatriotic, and even terrorist sympathizers. Dissenting voices were drowned out by a tidal wave of propaganda, all to ensure public support for the war effort. Dehumanization became a tool used to vilify not just the foreign enemy but also those at home who did not conform to the dominant narrative. Ultimately, this tactic is used to control narratives, influence perspectives, and sway public opinion.

Outright Deception

Those in power frequently lie to hide their evil deeds. One of the most insidious tools in the propaganda arsenal is outright deception, which leaves the public in a fog of uncertainty. In March 2013, then-Director of National Intelligence James Clapper testified to Congress about the activities of the National Security Agency (NSA). One senator asked him, "Does the NSA collect any type of data at all on millions or hundreds of millions of Americans?" Clapper responded, "No, sir... Not wittingly."[57] This was a blatant lie. Not only was the NSA collecting data on millions of Americans, but it was also doing so intentionally and systematically. This lie was thankfully exposed a few months later, when former NSA contractor Edward Snowden leaked thousands of documents detailing the NSA's extensive surveillance programs. Snowden's revelations shook the world and demonstrated the lengths to which those in power will go to keep their activities concealed and deceive the public.

Or consider the Tuskegee Syphilis Study, conducted between 1932 and 1972 by the US Public Health Service—a chilling testament to the depravity that can arise when those in power choose to deceive. In this egregious violation of human rights, hundreds of African American men were misled into believing they were receiving free healthcare while, in truth, they were subjects in a study observing the progression of untreated syphilis.[58] The men were never informed of their diagnosis, nor were they ever offered effective treatment, even after the discovery of penicillin as a cure for syphilis. The truth of this inhumane experiment only emerged forty years later, a stark reminder of the institutionalized deception capable of being perpetrated under the guise of public service.

What about Hunter Biden's laptop? Just before the 2020 presidential election, the *New York Post* published a story about Hunter Biden using his father's position and influence for personal gain—with his dad's knowledge and blessing. The *Post* had evidence to back up these claims, obtained from an abandoned laptop once owned by Hunter. But five days after the story, over fifty former intelligence community officials released a public statement suggesting the story was Russian disinformation. Pundits took the bait and ran with it, smearing anyone who believed the *Post* story. NPR called the story a "waste of time" and a "pure distraction."[59] But the laptop was authentic, and the *Post* story was fully accurate. These "intelligence" officers, using their high-ranking status to influence the public, were intentionally deceptive to help Joe Biden win the election.[60] The project was led by Michael Morell, acting director of the CIA, who was under consideration to be appointed as director if Biden won the election[61]—a clear incentive to deceive the public in hopes of gaining political power.

Influencers

As the old saying goes, "Birds of a feather flock together." That's the underlying principle of social proof, a potent psychological mechanism that compels us to follow the actions or beliefs of others. (It's why people look at reviews when considering a purchase—to see what others say before deciding for themselves.) After all, if others are doing it or believing in it, it must be correct or beneficial, right? This is especially true when the ones setting the example are those some people look up to or admire—"influencers" such as celebrities or public figures.

During COVID-19, there was a chorus of influential voices, from actors and musicians to politicians themselves, championing vaccination.[62] They received their jabs publicly, shared their vaccination experiences on social media, and encouraged followers to do the same. Their unified message was clear: "We got vaccinated; so should you." The collective weight of their influence was instrumental in shaping public opinion and encouraging vaccination uptake. Not that any of them were scientific experts, of course—but that didn't stop them from proclaiming to their followers that the experimental jab was definitely "safe and effective." Millions listened and obeyed—they were *influenced.*

Then there are election campaigns where celebrity endorsement is as common as the campaign promise itself. Remember when Hollywood's elite lined up to support Barack Obama or when a slew of celebrities rallied behind Donald Trump? These politicians leverage the popularity and star power of celebrities to boost their own standing and appeal.[63] Actors, musicians, and athletes support these politicians, lending them an air of trustworthiness and coolness. After all, if someone we admire supports a candidate, they can't be all bad, right?

But here's the catch. These influencers, whether they're celebrities endorsing a political candidate or a public figure advocating for a social cause or legal reform, are part of a larger propaganda machine. They often present a one-sided perspective, carefully curated to align with the narrative of those in power. Their messages lack nuance or critical thought, but that's the point—the bold messages use their status and charm to influence specific actions or beliefs among their adoring fans. This potent blend of influence and social proof is an age-old recipe for powerful propaganda, ensuring the message of those in power reverberates far and wide, echoed by the influential voices many know and trust.

BEWARE THE EXPERTS

John and Sally Sweek were stabbed to death inside their Dallas, Texas, apartment in 1987. As law enforcement officers began their investigation, an anonymous caller suggested they focus on Steven Chaney, who allegedly owed the Sweeks five hundred dollars.[1] Arrested by police a few days later, Chaney told investigators that he was working the day of the murders and had witnesses who could vouch for him. Despite that, prosecutors decided to charge Chaney with committing these murders, citing the testimony from two dentists who said bite marks on John Sweek's left arm matched Chaney's teeth. Relying on this expert testimony, a jury convicted Chaney, who was sentenced to life in prison.

For decades, Chaney argued that he was innocent of the crime. Using bite marks as evidence had similarly convicted scores of other defendants across the country, with expert witnesses testifying about their guilt based on their analysis of the bite marks. But as

science evolved, it became increasingly clear that this
wasn't science—it was junk science, or fraudulent evidence that is falsely claimed to be accurate or true.
In December 2018, the Court of Criminal Appeals in
Texas threw out Chaney's conviction. "Each piece of
the state's trial evidence is questionable or has since
been undermined or completely invalidated," the judges wrote.[2]

The experts—propped up by prosecutors as truth
tellers with advanced knowledge—were absolutely
wrong. In 2009, the National Academy of Sciences
published a report saying that matching bite marks to a
specific person had an "insufficient scientific basis."[3] In
other words, it wasn't possible. The "experts" made it
up! And their claims have had serious and even deadly
consequences for defendants who are falsely accused.
The National Registry of Exonerations has identified
553 cases since 1989 where a person was wrongfully
convicted using false or misleading forensic evidence.[4]

From medical misdiagnoses by expert medical
teams to faulty financial forecasts from expert econo-
mists, there are countless examples of people advanc-
ing their agenda by wrapping themselves in the cloak
of authority—after all, if they're the experts, then who
are we to question what they say? This becomes a powerful weapon in a mind war to neutralize others' de-

fenses; if a person can be propped up as an expert, then their recommendations or conclusions will more easily persuade those listening. But the public seems to be noticing that they are frequently lied to and manipulated by these "experts." A 2022 survey of American voters found that only 34 percent trust the mass media, such as newspapers, TV, and radio, when it comes to reporting the news fully and accurately.[5] Just 26 percent say they have a favorable view of the media.[6]

In general, how much trust and confidence do you have in the media — such as newspapers TV, and radio — when it comes to reporting the news fully and accurately?

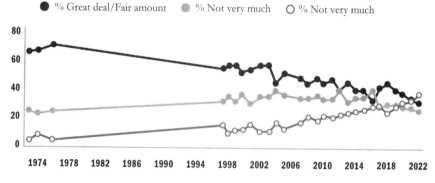

● % Great deal/Fair amount   ● % Not very much   ○ % Not very much

Americans' Trust in Mass Media, 1972-2022, Gallup

More interestingly, 50 percent of Americans believe that most national news organizations intend to mislead, misinform, or persuade the public.[7] And only 23 percent of Americans believe that these organizations care about the best interests of their readers, viewers, and listeners.[8] Fewer and fewer people trust pundits—or at least they say they don't. Yet when some new crisis emerges or a shocking event unfolds, most individuals believe what they are told because they lack any contrary information and fail to be initially skeptical about something that sounds so convincing. Without evidence, people often believe falsehoods pushed by the experts. Following the 9/11 attacks, President Bush and his associates insinuated that Saddam Hussein was somehow involved and that his weapons of mass destruction were linked to the event. They hoped the public ire over 9/11 would spill over into support for military intervention in Iraq, which many of Bush's allies had long desired. Months into the war, a reporter backed the president into a corner on the issue, leading Bush to reply, "We've had no evidence that Saddam Hussein was involved" with the 9/11 attacks. Despite the later denial, many Americans continued to believe the initial lies. Two years after the attacks, a *Washington Post* poll found that 69 percent of Americans believed Hussein was "personally" involved in the attacks, and 82 percent thought he had provided assistance to Osama bin Laden. Both were completely false.[9]

Those in power know that people are easily persuaded by those in authority, which is why experts are so often elevated and their views proclaimed as truth simply because they uttered them. And many of them abuse their position to push lies onto people. Francesca Gino, a prominent behavioral scientist at Harvard Business School, researches honesty. Her studies have been widely published and featured in a large number of news articles and broadcasts. She has received numerous awards for her work. And yet this honesty researcher was exposed for dishonesty, fraudulently altering data in her studies. Three other behavioral scientists dug into her work and "discovered evidence of fraud in papers spanning over a decade, including papers published quite recently."[10] This type of behavior rightly undermines people's trust in "experts" when it becomes clear that their beliefs can be manipulated through deception. Throughout the COVID-19 pandemic, for example, the people proclaimed as experts by friendly pundits pushed a wide range of falsehoods, including that masks helped stop the virus, that the Wuhan "lab leak" theory was a false conspiracy theory, and that the rushed vaccines would halt transmission of the virus between people. All of these were wrong, yet those who disagreed were branded as infidels for not "following the science." When people would point out that the experts were wrong, those experts would defensively dismiss their critics. Dr. Anthony

Fauci was perhaps the most prominent expert during the pandemic. He told an MSNBC host, "A lot of what you're seeing as attacks on me quite frankly are attacks on science, because all of the things that I have spoken about consistently from the very beginning, have been fundamentally based on science."[11] Fauci had pushed all the falsehoods mentioned above—about masks, the source of the virus, and the vaccines. He was consistently wrong yet claimed that those attacking him were "attacking science." How dare the commoners criticize the clergy!

To navigate today's mind wars, it's important to cultivate critical thinking, skepticism, and a constant quest for evidence-based knowledge. In an age where the voices of "experts" are amplified, people must recognize that truth is not established by how many acronyms you have after your name or how many years you studied in school. Truth is not derived from how many people agree with you or how loudly pundits will proclaim your words to a believing public. A thing is not true because somebody simply says it is—truth must be studied, challenged, and verified. Yet, many people become casualties in the mind war because they are easily deceived by the allure of authority. They put their trust in fallible and sometimes corrupt people who have their own biases and agenda that taint their beliefs and actions. If we're to survive the war and help save others, we need to recognize how these biases work, why experts can deceive, and why seeking the truth means being skeptical of unproven claims. Let's dive in.

EXPERTS ARE BIASED

Mika Brzezinski, a pundit on MSNBC, is among the many media voices who were vocal critics of President Donald Trump before, during, and after his time in office. On February 22, 2017, Brzezinski—whose father was previously the national security advisor and an outspoken academic—complained that Trump was "trying to undermine the media, he's trying to make up his own facts." She then said, "He could have undermined the messaging so much that he can actually control exactly what people think. And that, that is our job."[12]

This level of media manipulation and individual influence can't be achieved by pundits alone. They rely on experts—people whose views they agree with and whom they can cite as an authority figure. This allows pundits to mask their opinions behind the opinions of someone else they agree with—enabling them to push their agenda or convey their preferred views without being the one to do it directly. But these "experts" are simply people with opinions and perspectives. They're not unbiased sources who transparently tell the truth. And yet time and again, the public is manipulated into agreeing with the views of an expert because of the deceptive manner in which their opinions are cloaked as authoritative and accurate.

Countless examples could be shared to demonstrate this pattern. Let's pick on John Bolton. Formerly the national security advisor to President Trump and ambassador to the United Nations under President Bush, Bolton has a long career in government as an attorney, diplomat, and warmonger. Long before the 9/11 attacks and the Bush administration's efforts to deceive Americans into thinking Saddam Hussein had something to do with it, Bolton was an advocate of regime change in Iraq. He was the director for the Project for a New American Century—a group of pro-war advocates like him who wanted more American military presence in the Middle East. One of their reports, issued in 2000, stated that this military buildup would likely not happen unless the US experienced "a new Pearl Harbor," referencing the 1941 attack by the Japanese that galvanized public opinion and led the country into World War II. One year later, 9/11 happened, and Bolton and his allies, who were now in positions of power in President Bush's administration, were quick to initiate the plans they had long desired.

But the war they started was a disaster. There were no weapons of mass destruction. Saddam wasn't responsible for 9/11. And yet, these lies led to total chaos. In Iraq alone (ignoring all the other countries involved in the two decades of warfare), well over 100,000 Iraqis died, as well as 4,492 Americans.[13] Taxpayers were forced to spend over one trillion dollars for the war.[14] And for what? Iraq is not more peaceful or democratic than it was under Saddam's rule. His toppling led to a power vacuum that attracted different militant groups, such as the Islamic state. Before the US-led invasion of Iraq, there was no meaningful terrorist presence in the country, yet a decade later, a third of the country was controlled by terrorists.[15] Yet, Bolton argues that Iraq "suffers not from the 2003 invasion, but from the 2011 withdrawal of all US combat forces."[16] The obviously cruel sanctions imposed on Iraq—depriving people of food and medicine, causing an estimated one million Iraqi civilians to die[17]—were too lenient in Bolton's view; he thought there should have been "crushing sanctions... enforced cold-bloodedly."[18] Despite widespread consensus that the war was a wasteful failure predicated on lies, Bolton said two decades later, "Knowing everything I know now, I would do exactly the same thing."[19] This man has advocated for preemptive military strikes and wars against North Korea and Iran and seems to support any and all warfare possible[20]—even when evidence piles up showing how foolish and wrong such decisions might be.

He's extremely biased, driven by a pro-war agenda, and persistent in his advocacy of a foreign policy that leads to mass displacement and death. And yet, John Bolton is still propped up by the media as a foreign policy expert and regular commentator, despite having been so profoundly wrong about Iraq. And there are plenty of others who have "been wrong on nearly every major foreign policy and national security issue over the past four decades,"[21] as former defense secretary Robert Gates once said. Who was he referring to? President Joe Biden, who claimed that people refer to him as a "foreign policy expert!"[22] These people, like Bolton, are regularly given airtime by the largest media outlets across the country to share their "expertise" on geopolitical issues. Of course, war—like any controversy—is good for the media as it attracts attention (which brings in advertising revenue). Giving people like Bolton a platform, then, is not something that happens in spite of his bloodlust and bias—it's exactly *because* of it. That's why, as one writer put it, "Former intelligence officials are enjoying second acts as television pundits":

Former CIA Director John Brennan (2013-17) is the latest superspook to be reborn as a TV newsie. He just cashed in at NBC News as a "senior national security and intelligence analyst" and served his first expert views on last Sunday's edition of Meet the Press. The Brennan acquisition seeks to elevate NBC to spook parity with CNN, which employs former Director of National Intelligence James Clapper and former CIA Director Michael Hayden in a similar capacity. Other, lesser-known national security veterans thrive under TV's grow lights. Almost too numerous to list, they include Chuck Rosenberg, former acting DEA administrator, chief of staff for FBI Director James B. Comey, and counselor to former FBI Director Robert S. Mueller III; Frank Figliuzzi, former chief of FBI counterintelligence; Juan Zarate, deputy national security adviser under Bush, at NBC; and Fran Townsend, homeland security adviser under Bush, at CBS News. CNN's bulging roster also includes former FBI agent Asha Rangappa; former FBI agent James Gagliano; Obama's former deputy national security adviser Tony Blinken; former House Intelligence Committee Chairman Mike Rogers; senior adviser to the National Security Council during the Obama administration Samantha Vinograd; retired CIA operations officer Steven L. Hall; and Philip Mudd, also retired from the CIA.[23]

All of these people—all of them—are extremely biased. Sure, they're experienced, but they are dedicated
to a particular viewpoint. This agenda-driven infil-
tration into the media used to be done covertly, as in
the case of Operation Mockingbird. Not anymore. But
don't think this just applies to issues like geopolitics
and war. Every topic has its "experts" whose opinions
are elevated and pushed onto the masses because it's
profitable for the politicians and pundits. It happens
in climate science, economics, public health, sports,
finance, and more. Laughably, those who are often
the most biased try to pass themselves off as impartial truth tellers. They dismiss contrary viewpoints as
"misinformation," implicitly elevating their own ideas
as accurate and impartial "information" by comparison.

This movement gained so much traction that in
2022, the Department of Homeland Security created a
Disinformation Governance Board to respond to ideas
and claims that affect "public trust in our democratic institutions"[24]—as if the public needs the government to tell them what is true and what is false! The
woman tapped to run this institution, Nina Jankowicz,
was dubbed an "expert on disinformation"[25] by media
outlets favorable to her political views. Her boss said
she was "eminently qualified, a renowned expert in
the field of disinformation."[26] And what was her pro-

fessional background that qualified her to be branded as an arbiter of truth? She obtained a college degree in "Russian, Eurasian, and East European Studies," worked at the National Democracy Institute for International Affairs, was a commentator for progressive media outlets, and wrote a book. None of this qualifies her to be such an "expert." Indeed, her actual positions show she was and is an activist—a highly biased, agenda-driven individual. She once advocated that Twitter should allow verified users to edit others' tweets if they felt they were misleading. She spread doubt about the *New York Post*'s accurate reporting on Hunter Biden's laptop, calling the attention a "Trump campaign product" fabricated to help him win re-election. This was, of course, completely false. She also claimed that Trump had ties to the Kremlin-linked Alfa-Bank, an allegation that many other left-leaning "experts" repeated to try and paint their political foe in a negative light. This, too, was completely false. As Glenn Greenwald once wrote, "Anyone bestowing upon themselves the term 'disinformation expert' should be assumed to be a fraud, almost certainly an operative to *disseminate* disinformation, not combat it."[27] Indeed, Jankowicz was not an unbiased truth teller combating falsehoods in the name of fighting disinformation. She was actually a purveyor of untruth, a partisan extremist spreading

the very thing she claimed to be fighting. Greenwald
continued:

> What is a "disinformation expert"?
>
> Does it require a particular degree? Is there
> some licensing board or official certification is-
> sued? What credentials, scholarship or accom-
> plishments are needed to justify someone being
> lavished with this pompous label?
>
> Just as media corporations re-branded their
> partisan pundits as "fact-checkers"—to mas-
> querade their opinions as elevated, apolitical
> authoritative, decrees of expertise—the term
> "disinformation expert" is designed to disguise
> ideological views as Official Truth.
>
> It's a scam.[28]

The term *expert* is now meaningless, especially in
the post-pandemic era after supposed experts repeatedly claimed the vaccines were safe and effective, masks
helped slow the spread of COVID-19, shutting down the
economy was necessary, etc. It has become apparent that
the term is a weaponized label applied to those whose
views are sanctioned and supported by those in power.
It is a means to propagandize the public into believing a
claim simply because of the authoritative position of an
expert. And worse of all, the term is audaciously used to

prop a person up as being unbiased and neutral—someone who is credible and should be believed by others, especially those who don't already agree with them. Without any apparent shame, the media will tell you to trust the experts all while quoting and highlighting the experts who have been consistently wrong about every major prediction and issue over the last several decades. So, see the experts for what they are—biased individuals with an agenda and opinions that are favorable to the politicians and pundits giving them a platform. Even if that expert is wearing a lab coat.

DECEIVERS IN LAB COATS

On a sunny morning in October 2009, 150 doctors sat in closely packed chairs on the White House lawn, summoned by President Barack Obama's administration to be in the front rows of the orchestrated audience. Earlier that year, Obama had announced his proposed healthcare reforms, dubbed "Obamacare," and had pursued multiple methods to get Congress to pass them into law. The doctors-turned-props for this media spectacle were notified in their invitation to "Wear your white lab coat"[29]—a visual representation for the captured TV footage, so viewers would understand who they were. But many of them forgot, "failing to meet the White House dress code by showing up in business suits or dresses. So the White House rustled up white coats for them and handed them to the suited physicians, who had taken seats in the sun-splashed lawn area."[30]

Four doctors were selected to stand behind the President, so the visual effect would be seen from every angle of the captured footage. Surrounded by these physicians who supported his proposal, President Obama told the assembled audience, "Nobody has more credibility with the American people on this issue than you do."[31] Leaning into this supposed support from the medical community, Obama added, "Some of the people who are most supportive of reform are the very medical professionals who know the healthcare system best."[32]

President Barack Obama pitches his health care plan surrounded by doctors in white lab coats, October 5, 2009

And that's why the lab coats were ordered—because of the powerful status symbol they were to subconsciously signify to viewers that "doctors support Obamacare." That was the main message to be delivered to the viewing audience, regardless of whatever flowery speech the President was giving. Obama's team knew that people generally trust their doctors (at least in the days before COVID-19[33]), and that for decades, the white lab coat has been a symbol associated with these physicians that conveys trust, intelligence, and authority. But this garment served no practical purpose for any of these physicians attending the White House press event. They weren't in a lab or office; they weren't seeing patients. It was purely a form of propaganda designed to evoke an emotion.

In Obama's case, the White House treated these physicians like puppets, pulling their strings for visual effect to try and create political support for their healthcare reforms. But doctors don't just don a lab coat when requested for a photo op—they know the power of this symbol, and they use it to their own advantage to encourage others to see them as an expert. Consider the example of Dr. Vin Gupta, a pulmonologist (lung doctor) and medical analyst for MSNBC, who pundits claimed to be "a high-profile public health expert."[34] Throughout the COVID-19 ordeal, Gupta fanatically hyped the fear of this virus on television, at one point suggesting that those who didn't receive the vaccine should be denied access to major medical treatments as a punishment.[35] But as the pandemic waned, Gupta's fear mongering continued. In one case, he appeared on MSNBC to warn that "climate change" could lead to another pandemic because of "unnatural migration patterns, closer proximity to other mammals, like humans, and you're seeing that [virus] transmission become more and more common."[36] With the title "Global Health Policy Expert" boldly displayed along the bottom of the screen, Gupta spoke to viewers while dressed in a white lab coat—not because it was required by others or practical in any way, but because he wanted to leverage its symbolic effect on the human mind in order to make his views more credible.

Whether it's a lab coat, a fancy title, some initials after your name, a military uniform, or some other credential or costume, there are a number of ways in which someone's views can get a leg up simply because of who they are perceived to be. That was certainly the case for Paul Ehrlich, a well-known biologist from Stanford University. Ehrlich was interviewed for *60 Minutes* in early 2023 to convince viewers of an impending environmental disaster of epic proportions. But Ehrlich has been wrong throughout his entire career. In 1970, he said, "I and the vast majority of my colleagues think we've had it; that the next few decades will be the end of the kind of civilization we're used to," and, "Humanity is very busily sitting on a limb that we're sawing off."[37] Then Ehrlich said, "In ten years all important animal life in the sea will be extinct. Large areas of coastline will have to be evacuated because of the stench of dead fish."[38] Pretty startling stuff, right? Statements like this were believed by many because he shot to fame as a scientific expert on population after writing *The Population Bomb* in 1968. In that book, Ehrlich wrote:

> The battle to feed all of humanity is over. In the 1970s and 1980s hundreds of millions of people will starve to death in spite of any crash programs embarked upon now. At this late date nothing can prevent a substantial increase in the world death rate, although many lives could be saved through dramatic programs to "stretch" the carrying capacity of the earth by increasing food production and providing for more equitable distribution of whatever food is available. But these programs will only provide a stay of execution unless they are accompanied by determined and successful efforts at population control. Population control is the conscious regulation of the numbers of human beings to

meet the needs not just of individual families, but of society as a whole.

Nothing could be more misleading to our children than our present affluent society. They will inherit a totally different world, a world in which the standards, politics, and economics of the past decade are dead. As the most influential nation in the world today, and its largest consumer, the United States cannot stand isolated. We are today involved in the events leading to famine and ecocatastrophe; tomorrow we may be destroyed by them.[39]

These wild claims turned out, of course, to be completely false. But long before *60 Minutes* gave Ehrlich continued credibility as an expert commentator, he was filling the airwaves with other nonsensical claims. In 1970, he predicted that by 1999, the population of all of North America would be a measly 22.6 million,[40] when in reality it ended up being over 405 million. In that same year, relying on his belief that overpopulation would decimate the world, he suggested that the government should make sure "large families are always treated in a negative light on television" and to "legislate the size of the family," throwing a parent in jail "if you have too many kids."[41] The following year, he claimed that "England will not exist in the year 2000"[42] as a result of too many humans using up too few resources. Again and again and again, his predictions failed to materialize—he was consistently wrong.[43] And yet the pundits at CBS continued to cite him as an expert on the matter, despite decades of failed predictions of doom and gloom.

Scientific progress is built on the premise of challenging and refining ideas, yet many "experts" instead use their privileged position to ignore and attack anyone who questions their view. Dr. Peter Hotez is one such deceiver, a fierce proponent of the COVID-19 vaccines, who argued that the United Nations should "dismantle anti-vaccine groups in the United States" because expressing skepticism about these injectable products was, in his view, "anti-science" that "requires a counteroffensive."[44] He chased every camera that would interview him—knowing that the pundits would only ask easy questions—often wearing his signature lab coat while decrying as "misinformation" anyone who challenged his claims that the vaccines were safe and effective. But when podcaster Joe Rogan challenged Hotez to a debate on the topic against presidential candidate and vaccine skeptic Robert F. Kennedy, Jr., the supposed "expert" would not dignify his adversary's views by sharing a platform with him. Over $2 million was pledged to charity to entice Hotez to engage,[45] yet he refused because he felt that "doing so would provide anti-vaxxers like Kennedy with an opportunity to spread their baseless views even further."[46] This is like saying, "The issue is beneath me to discuss with you... but you must comply with my views." And it's not science—science is the challenging and refining of ideas through open inquiry and debate. Instead, it's authoritarian propaganda where questioning the consensus leads to censorship or dismissal; dissenting voices become marginalized or silenced by the propagandists, politicians, and pundits—even when their critiques are valid and factually correct.

Experts are powerful weapons in a mind war; before even speaking, people are conditioned to feel and think in certain ways as a result of an expert's appearance or title. Someone who is interested in communicating the truth, knowing these faults of the human brain, will downplay his appearance and title to let his words and ideas be subject to scrutiny and debate. But activists pushing an agenda—soldiers in the war on your mind—will exploit them to their fullest. The human mind, inherently susceptible to the influence of perceived authority, often yields unquestioning obedience to those donned in the garb of expertise, title, or status. Whether it's the white lab coat of a doctor, the uniform of a soldier, or the credentials of a scholar, people subconsciously associate these symbols with authority, and, subsequently, trustworthiness. And as a result, powerful people use such experts in order to deceive, knowing that the masses will be swayed as a result of these symbols. Our challenge, then, is to cultivate a discerning mind capable of distinguishing between genuine expertise and cunningly crafted facades of authority. And there is a tool people can rely on to filter out deception and find the truth: replication.

TRUTH IS REPLICABLE

After Paul Ehrlich appeared on *60 Minutes*, many critics took to social media to highlight his decades-long record of false predictions. *Reason* magazine wrote that the TV show "should be ashamed of promoting perennial doomster Paul Ehrlich's failed predictions of civilizational collapse yet one more time."[47] Investigative journalist Michael Shellenberger highlighted the contradiction in Ehrlich's position, noting that Ehrlich claimed in the interview that global warming would lead to mass famine, despite having claimed half a century ago that global *cooling* would have the same result.[48] In response to widespread criticism and the surfacing of his failed predictions to the public's consciousness, Ehrlich rose to his defense with this comment:

> If I'm always wrong, so is science, since my
> work is always peer-reviewed, including the
> *Population Bomb* and I've gotten virtually every
> scientific honor. Sure I've made some mistakes,
> but no basic ones.[49]

One wonders why someone so consistently wrong
has "gotten virtually every scientific honor," but what's
really striking is what Ehrlich says at the beginning: if
he's always wrong, then *so is science*. And the reason why
he believes this? "My work is always peer-reviewed."
When someone makes an observation or conducts an
experiment, they can submit their research by writing
a paper for publication in a scientific journal. The editor of that journal sends the paper to two or three other
researchers who were not involved in the experiment to
review the paper, looking for any mistakes or problems.
If things look right to them, they give their stamp of approval for publication. Ehrlich relies on this process to
claim that his views are scientifically correct—as if passing through peer review (and getting two or three others to agree with you) establishes whether something is
true. The danger with relying on the peer-review process as an indicator of truth is that the "experts" often
become part of an echo chamber where they agree with
one another unquestioningly, whether believing that
climate change is caused by humans[50] or that bloodlet-

ting can help improve someone's poor health[51] or that
smoking cigarettes is good for you.[52] Truth is not established by a vote or a majority or by having a few people
agree with you.

In 1996, three researchers published their peer-
reviewed study in the *Journal of Personality and Social
Psychology* titled "Automaticity of social behavior."[53]
In this experiment, researchers had thirty-four students complete a brief research task to observe the effect it had on them. Students were presented with a
scrambled sentence, such as *they her respect see usually*.
Some students were given sentences that contained
polite words, while others were given words related to
rudeness. The researchers observed that the students
who unscrambled sentences about rudeness were
more likely to interrupt the conversation than those
whose sentences were about politeness.[54] They called
this effect *priming*—conditioning a person to act in a
certain way by first exposing the individual to a stereotype or concept. But there was a second act in the
experiment; some of the students had been exposed
to scrambled sentences with words related to elderly
people, whereas others were not. After students were
told the experiment was over and left the laboratory,
researchers monitored the speed at which the students
were walking, finding that the students exposed to the

elderly priming walked more slowly than the others, consistent with the stereotype about old people.[55]

This study has been cited over 5,000 times by other researchers and is regularly featured in psychology textbooks to help students learn about how priming works. In 2011, Nobel Prize-winning psychologist Daniel Kahneman authored a book, *Thinking Fast and Slow*, in which he referred to this study and wrote, "Disbelief is not an option. The results are not made up, nor are they statistical flukes. You have no choice but to accept that the major conclusions of these studies are true."[56] So a team of independent researchers decided to challenge that declaration. The following year, they tried running the exact same experiment but found no differences in the walking speed of students, despite only some being primed with elderly words. Another researcher tried five times to replicate the priming results without success.[57] This incident sparked a "replication crisis"—a widespread questioning of how accurate psychological research has been despite being published in peer-reviewed journals. To save the reputation of their profession, many psychologists teamed up to recreate famous and well-established experiments—research that had long been accepted as true. In one such effort, only half of peer-reviewed psychological studies could be repeated successfully.[58] Even

the successful replications found that the original studies had exaggerated the significance of their findings.

No one knows for sure just how widespread these
failures are because not everything is being retested.
Hal Pashler is one of the psychologists who failed to
replicate the priming results. He pointed out that scientists aren't incentivized to point out failed replication attempts since this type of work opens them up to
criticism from colleagues and doesn't advance their own
publication record. Pashler calls it the "file-drawer problem," where "studies with negative results get shoved
into psychologists' file drawers, never to be shared or
published."[59] But the replication crisis doesn't just apply
to psychology: a 2016 attempt to replicate eighteen economic studies only had a 61 percent rate;[60] a 2018 neuroscience review of brain-imaging studies found that
the results were only "modestly replicable";[61] and "low
reproducibility has been recognized as an issue in ecology and evolution for a long time, but little has been done
to confront it."[62] Across scientific professions, the peer-
reviewed publications that Ehrlich extolled are subject
to very little replication. In economics, for example,
only 0.1 percent of journal articles published were replication attempts of past studies, and studies published in
the top five economics journals had an even lower replication rate.[63] Psychology replication was roughly ten

times better than economics, but still, just over one percent of studies had attempted replications.[64] This means that there are a vast number of studies and experiments that are assumed to be true—because they were peer-reviewed, as if that means much—yet we simply don't know because no one has attempted to replicate them. Imagine someone attempting to replicate every study that has ever been done—what percentage do you think would actually be repeatable?

In 2016, comedian John Oliver dedicated a portion of his *Last Week Tonight* show to this issue, showcasing flashy claims by media pundits about what science supposedly showed. "A new study shows how sugar might feed the growth of cancer," one reporter said. "A new study shows late night snacking could damage the part of your brain that creates and stores memories," read another from her teleprompter. Another one: "A new study finds pizza is the most addictive food in America." Or "A new study suggests hugging your dog is bad for your dog." And "A new study shows that drinking a glass of red wine is just as good as spending an hour at the gym." Oliver observed, "After a certain point, all that ridiculous information can make you wonder, is science bullsh—?"[65] There have been a number of similarly flashy headlines and popular claims based off of some researchers' peer-reviewed, published research. For example:

- Professor Brian Wansink, the head of Cornell University's Food and Brand Lab, published a 2005 study called "Super Bowls: Serving Bowl Size and Food Consumption," in which he claimed that study participants serving themselves food from large bowls took 53 percent more food and consumed 56 percent more of it than those who served themselves from small bowls.[66] In an article titled "Your Plate Is Bigger Than Your Stomach," the *New York Times* praised Wansink's work and wrote conclusively, "Large plates and bowls lead to more eating [because] they make portions look smaller."

- "New Study Finds Eggs Will Break Your Heart," said the Physicians Committee for Responsible Medicine in 2019. Countless pundits echoed this announcement, telling their viewers that "Americans are eating 279 eggs per person a year, and a new study finds it's killing them."[67] The underlying study was published in the *Journal for the American Medical Association* and claimed that "higher consumption of dietary cholesterol or eggs was significantly associated with higher risk of incident cardiovascular disease and all-cause mortality."[68]

- Matthew Walker, a professor at the University of California, Berkeley, wrote a book called *Why We Sleep* that soon became a bestseller; his companion TED talk got millions of views. Walker taught that science suggests everyone should get eight hours of sleep per night, otherwise, we suffer negative health consequences. "Routinely sleeping less than six or seven hours a night demolishes your immune system, more than doubling your risk of cancer," he wrote.[69]

All of these are wrong. Wansink's research was retracted, and he retired from his university position after people started looking into his other research, finding it full of holes.[70] Eggs don't cause cardiovascular disease; the data used for the research had a "serious measurement error."[71] And what's more, "There also seems to be a number of nutrients found in eggs that seem to *inhibit* cholesterol absorption!"[72] And the supposed sleep doctor butchered the science; there are no studies "that would reasonably be able to establish causality, that would support this claim."[73] Writing about these and more bogus claims that are regularly spread by the scientific community, Stuart Ritchie, author of *Science Fictions: How Fraud, Bias, Negligence, and Hype Undermine the Search for Truth*, wrote:

Science, the discipline in which we should find the harshest skepticism, the most pin-sharp rationality and the hardest-headed empiricism, has become home to a dizzying array of incompetence, delusion, lies and self-deception.[74]

Contrary to Ehrlich's claims, the peer-review process is not sufficient to establish truth. Despite churning out all kinds of unreplicated, or worse, unreplicable (and thus untrue) research, so-called scientific experts are still regularly trusted by the masses; 83 percent of Americans surveyed in 2018 said that they trusted scientists, and 85 percent trusted science more broadly.[75] (These numbers ticked up by a few percentage points during the COVID-19 pandemic.) All this to say, experts are routinely wrong despite being trusted, and the research upon which they base their views is often riddled with inaccuracies and outright falsehoods. Truth is replicable—people shouldn't need to base their views and understanding of the world on the claims of a few peer-reviewed papers. Don't believe everything you read, even in a scholarly publication; there's a chance the study was funded by someone who wanted a particular outcome in order to persuade you to believe something that benefited them.

BRAIN PAIN

In the spring of 1953, the Korean War was about to conclude, leading to the division of Korea into a north and south side—the north being controlled by Communists. Joseph Stalin, the dictator leading the Soviet Union, had just died. And in the United States, Dwight D. Eisenhower—the famed Army general who served as Supreme Commander of the Allied Expeditionary Force in Europe during World War II—had just assumed office as president of the country. During the war, Eisenhower relied on intelligence briefings from the Office of Strategic Services (OSS) to understand what was happening behind enemy lines. But his chief of staff was curious about how these intelligence activities fit into the military, prompting the head of the OSS to write a letter to President Franklin D. Roosevelt. The memo stressed the post-war need for a "Central Intelligence Service... which will procure intelligence both by overt and covert methods" and conduct "subversive operations abroad."[1] In other words, intelligence gathering was not to be simply a wartime affair—the government needed an ongoing ability to monitor and influence others.

As the war concluded and before Eisenhower rose to power, President Harry S. Truman set out to dismantle the government offices that had been created to fight the war, and the OSS was on the chopping block. At its peak, employing almost 13,000 people, the entire office was dissolved over the course of ten days.[2] Soon after, Congress passed the National Security Act of 1947, which created the Central Intelligence Agency (CIA), a peacetime intelligence office to do what the OSS had recommended just a few years prior. Once in office in 1953, Eisenhower had to appoint a wide range of officials to various offices, including the position of CIA director. For that, he turned to Allen Dulles, a deputy director at the agency whom Eisenhower favored. With this appointment, Dulles became the first civilian director of the CIA.

Six weeks after being appointed, Dulles spoke to the alumni of his alma mater, Princeton University. Responding to widespread concern about the Soviet Union, Dulles warned his audience that the Communist nation was conducting a new "mind control" program. "Its aim" he said, "is to condition the mind so that it no longer reacts on a free will or rational basis but responds to impulses implanted from outside."[3] He continued:

> If we are to counter this kind of warfare, we must understand the techniques the Soviet is adopting to control men's minds...

> The human mind is the most delicate of all instruments. It is so finely adjusted, so susceptible to the impact of outside influences that it is proving a malleable tool in the hands of sinister men... We in the West are somewhat handicapped in brain warfare.[4]

Dulles further claimed, "It is hard for us to realize that in the great area behind the Iron Curtain a vast experiment is underway to change men's minds, working on them continuously from youth to old age."[5]

Imagine yourself in that audience, learning from this high-ranking government official about a mind-manipulation program being conducted by crazy Communists half a world away. You'd no doubt be shocked and appalled, criticizing these nefarious Marxists for their authoritarian activities. You'd return home from listening to this speech and likely share the news with family and friends. For weeks, it would gnaw at you— the idea that evil people around the world were coming up with ways to control the minds of their victims. But what you wouldn't know is that just three days after the speech, Dulles secretly ordered his spy agency to enter the mind-control business as well. So much for being "somewhat handicapped"...

Known as Project MK-Ultra, this top-secret government program involved mind-control experiments using drugs, electroshock therapy, toxins, hypnosis, radiation, and more. Some participants had volunteered freely for the program, but most were enrolled under coercion or without any knowledge that they were human guinea pigs for the CIA's activities. Soldiers, prisoners, mentally impaired individuals, and other vulnerable members of society were lab rats for Dulles's project. While governments had long sought to engineer consent through changing popular opinion, now they were turning to weaponizing science and psychology to coerce consent by reengineering the human brain. Dulles attacked the "sinister men" in the Soviet Union for doing this, mere moments before directly overseeing mind-control experiments at levels that dwarfed anything being done by the Soviets.

Even worse, those carrying out this vast experiment concluded that "unwitting [participants] would be desirable." For over a decade, MK-Ultra involved 149 projects using drug experimentation and other tactics, often on unsuspecting individuals. To avoid scrutiny, the CIA set up secret detention facilities in areas under American control, such as in Japan, Germany, and the Philippines, so that they could avoid criminal prosecution if they were discovered. CIA officers captured people suspected of being "enemy agents" and other people they felt were expendable and began experimenting on and torturing them. These prisoners were interrogated while being given drugs, shocked with electricity, and subjected to extremes of temperature and sensory isolation.

Crazy, right? And you might think that in the "land of the free," there would be some kind of oversight or accountability to shut down this program and hold those responsible accountable. Traditionally, that's the role of an inspector general—an independent government employee who reviews, audits, and makes transparent the activities of the agency they oversee. In this case, quite the opposite happened. A 1963 report from the CIA's inspector general says this:

> Precautions must be taken not only to protect operations from exposure to enemy forces but also to conceal these activities from the American public in general. The knowledge that the [CIA] is engaging in unethical and illicit activities would have serious repercussions in political and diplomatic circles and would be detrimental to the accomplishment of its mission. [6]

Corrupt governments have long used propaganda to persuade their citizens to support what leaders propose. These tactics are used to encourage support for a war, an election campaign, a bailout program, a pandemic response, and a host of other situations. Like Edward Bernays once said, "The engineering of consent is the very essence of the democratic process, the freedom to persuade and suggest."[7] But the methods used by Project MK-Ultra represent a far more sophisticated and nefarious approach to the "engineering of consent." Whereas propaganda typically relies on the written or spoken word to plant ideas in a person's mind, the CIA's conspiratorial mind-control program sought ways to use chemical and behavioral modification to alter a person's perceptions and actions.

In today's mind war, our brains are our primary weapon to fight back against the enemy. We rely upon our rational faculties to understand reality, determine the truth, and combat error. But our brains are also our chief vulnerability—our psychological Achilles' heel that exposes us to attacks from the enemy. For that reason, it is critical that we understand how our brains work, so we can minimize our vulnerabilities and better fight the enemy. Remember, Bernays said those who "understand the mental processes... of the masses" are the ones "who pull the wires which control the public mind."[8] If we don't understand how the brain works—and how it's so susceptible to control—then we will become an easy casualty in the mind war.

THE FOLLIES OF YOUTH

Aurora Casilli began working as a fourteen-year-old, saving up as much as she possibly could to one day afford her dream home. By age eighteen, she had saved just over $25,000—at one point, working three jobs to earn even more—and then lost it all. "I'm devastated. I've worked hard all my life," she told a reporter when sharing the story of how she lost the money.[9] Just as she became a legal adult, Aurora received a text message from her bank alerting her that someone with an unfamiliar name was attempting to make a transfer from her account. She promptly called the phone number listed in the text and followed the instructions of the bank employee, who told her she needed to create a new account and transfer her funds in order to ensure their protection. But the text wasn't her bank, and the employee was not an authorized agent with custody of Aurora's funds. It was a spoof text designed to scam unsuspecting people into sending their money to the thieves. The person she spoke with "sounded like any normal person working at a bank," Aurora explained. "You hear things on the news about scammers being from other countries and having broken English or heavy foreign accents. But he... spoke in a professional way. It did not seem suspicious."[10]

While scams like this happen to a large number of individuals, younger people are typically more susceptible. According to the Federal Bureau of Investigation, in 2021 nearly 15,000 scams were reported by teenagers, resulting in losses of over $100 million.[11] Predators use a variety of tactics to target unsuspecting youngsters; bank spoofing like Aurora experienced is only one method. Fraudsters will create fake employment offers and offer people remote positions with a hefty paycheck with the goal of harvesting the recruit's personal information in an identity-theft scheme in order to open new bank accounts, forge documents, etc.[12] And far darker activities like human trafficking[13] and sextortion[14] prey on young people who lack the experience and knowledge necessary to avoid falling into deeply troubling traps. There's also the silly—but potentially lethal—trends like the "Tide Pod challenge,"[15] where countless teenagers, enticed by social media attention, began eating Tide detergent pods on camera to get a reaction out of others (and hopefully a "like, subscribe, and share").

Understanding the teenage brain can help us realize how vulnerable young people can be to fraudsters and predators—whether they are thieves, traffickers, and social media influencers, or propagandists, politicians, and pundits. Research suggests that during adolescence an "increased interest in peer relationships" develops along with heightened "susceptibility to peer influence," which peaks around age 14.[16] At this stage of development, the brain makes adolescents more sensitive to the rewards these relationships produce than adults experience. This can help explain why teens might be more likely to consume laundry detergent to get a reaction from their peers than someone twice their age might be. To demonstrate this, researchers created a simulated driving experiment using people of various ages, all of whom performed similarly when driving alone. But when the subjects of the experiment were paired with two friends their age in the simulation, teenagers were more likely to engage in risky driving; for adults, the presence of friends had no impact.

Two aspects of the brain reveal why this difference occurred. First up are the amygdala and the striatum—two portions of the human brain that affect decision-making. The two amygdalae in your brain help regulate emotional responses, and the striatum helps control the reward system, which releases a chemical that makes you feel good, signifying that the relevant action was a positive one. Due to an increased amount of hormones during the teen years, these areas of the brain are flooded with receptors for oxytocin—a chemical that fosters prosocial behavior like bonding with others.[17] These neurological changes "make teens more focused on the rewards of peers and being included in peer activities,"[18] which helps explain why the driving simulation saw different results for this age group compared to adults. In fact, brain scans conducted during the experiment showed that teenagers "used areas of the brain that are more closely associated with rewards."[19] But not so for the adults. Whereas the juveniles' brain scans showed heavy activity in the reward centers of the brain, adults in the experiment showed heavy activity in the prefrontal cortex—the brain's control center for rational decision-making and self-control, helping regulate our impulses. This area of the brain is not mature and fully functioning until around age 25,[20] depriving younger people of the self-regulation abilities that adults enjoy.

Beyond brain issues, young people fall prey to others because they simply lack experience to know any better. The familiar saying "Those who don't learn from the past are condemned to repeat it" makes intuitive sense, but if someone hasn't been taught the past—or been alive long enough to have experienced it themselves—then they are subject to making mistakes or going down the wrong path. Youthful inexperience is why adolescents have a naturally high interest in exploration and novelty-seeking—trying to make sense of the world, gaining new knowledge and insights, and becoming more confident as they navigate new environments. They are trying to sift through competing ideas and form their worldview, bombarded at every turn by authority figures—parents, teachers, politicians, influencers, clergy, and more—who want to persuade (or propagandize) them. The teenage brain is malleable and flexible, allowing for easier adaptation to new ideas or information.[21] In such a dynamic environment and without the experience to wisely separate fact from fiction, teenagers can be prone to making bad decisions and falling prey to traps placed by others.

The impressionability of the young mind is precisely why dictators and despots throughout world history created programs and propaganda to cultivate their loyalty. Trained from a young age to trust authority, children are likely to swallow information they're spoon-fed by predators; they lack the ability to psychologically resist. In a November 1933 speech, Adolf Hitler revealed the playbook shared by other megalomaniacs:

> When an opponent declares, "I will not come over to your side," I calmly say, "Your child be-

longs to us already... What are you? You will pass on. Your descendants, however, now stand in the new camp. In a short time they will know nothing else but this new community.[22]

Years later, he said, "This new Reich will give its youth to no one, but will itself take youth and give to youth its own education and its own upbringing."[23] He verbalized the core totalitarian belief, that of capturing children's minds to secure the future of the state. Parents be damned—they would "pass on," as Hitler pointed out, and expire along with their allegedly antiquated views and loyalties. In their place would rise the new generation, educated and cultivated in a way that aligns with the approval of those in power. In North Korea, children are taught "never to forget that they owed everything to the national leadership."[24] Vladimir Lenin revealed why schools in the Soviet Union had a "political function... to construct communist society" when he said, "Our work in the sphere of education is part of the struggle for the overthrow of the bourgeoisie. We publicly declare that education divorced from life and politics is a lie and hypocrisy."[25] For these and other authoritarian thugs, children were raw material to be exploited for their political goals.

This type of mind war is not relegated to foreign countries, evil dictators, or the pages of history. It is found in schools across the United States of America as well, and this outcome is not a flaw in the system. It is the core feature—the intent for which the system's early pioneers created it. Consider Horace Mann, who first institutionalized modern schooling in Massachusetts in 1837. "Men are cast-iron," he wrote, "but children are wax."[26] Even from this early era, those in power recognized how malleable the minds of young children were compared to the stubborn resistance of adults. Mann and his colleagues traveled to Prussia—the German empire—to learn from their new model of education that focused on creating obedient and compliant soldiers and citizens. They appreciated the authoritarian model that relied on top-down management and instruction, treating each child as a cog in a machine—to be molded as they designed. But many families failed to enroll their children in school, so Mann and his allies created the country's first compulsory schooling law in 1852 to require attendance under threat of punishing the parents. Capturing the minds of some of the young was insufficient—they needed to influence the entire rising generation to fulfill their goals. And parents were the threat; Mann told his colleagues that they should "look upon all parents as having given hostages to our cause."[27] Those aren't the words of someone providing an unbiased education to enrich a child's life. They are the words of a predator fighting a mind war.

ADULTS AREN'T IMMUNE

Adolf Hitler's aggressive outreach to the youth—even criminalizing competing organizations to monopolize the rising generation into the Hitler Youth program—was a bold move to capture the minds of millions of children. But the Nazis aimed their propaganda at everyone, not just juveniles. The entire citizenry was subjected to Goebbels' efforts, unspared from the relentless messaging that pushed the party message. And yet the approach for adults was somewhat similar to how propaganda was produced; Hitler wrote in Mein Kampf, "The broad masses of the people are not made up of... persons who are able to form reasoned judgment in given cases, but a vacillating crowd of human children who are constantly wavering between one idea and another."[28] He saw the public at large as foolish and ignorant.

Was Hitler right? Was this true? It's something that Milton Mayer wondered about. Mayer was a Jewish American journalist of German descent who interviewed a variety of Germans with different backgrounds and circumstances to better understand how Nazism became a mass movement. By the end of his project, Mayer observed that he could "see a little better how Nazism overcame Germany—not by attack from without or by subversion from within, but with a whoop and a holler."[29]

> It was what most Germans wanted—or, under pressure of combined reality and illusion, came to want. They wanted it; they got it; and they liked it.

> I came back home a little afraid for my country, afraid of what it might want, and get, and like, under pressure of combined reality and illusion. I felt—and feel—that it was not German Man that I had met, but Man. He happened to be in Germany under certain conditions. He might be here, under certain conditions. He might, under certain conditions, be I.[30]

One of Mayer's interviewees told him that the propaganda "took place so gradually and so insensibly, each step disguised (perhaps not even intentional) as a temporary emergency measure or associated with true patriotic allegiance or with real social purposes. And all the crises and reforms so occupied the people that they did not see the slow motion underneath..."[31] Person after person—all of them adults—shared with Mayer how they had been manipulated and how they had suppressed their conscience to go along with the new order of things.

So, too, with the soldiers themselves—party members and government officials who carried out Hitler's wishes, committing barbarous acts. Twenty-four of them were put on trial for war crimes at Nuremberg. The soldiers defended their actions by passing the blame up the chain of command, saying that they were "just following orders." A decade and a half later, that justification was again used in the case of Adolf Eichmann, who directly oversaw the logistics required to deport millions of Jewish men, women, and children to ghettos and extermination camps. Eichmann had evaded capture at the war's conclusion, fleeing to Argentina using false papers. He was kidnapped by Israeli agents in 1960, relocated to Israel, and, like the soldiers at Nuremberg fifteen years earlier, charged with war crimes and crimes against humanity. Eichmann's trial was widely televised, in part to educate the public about the crimes committed against Jews. One of the many people who watched the trial unfold was Stanley Milgram, a social psychologist at Yale. He wondered whether Eichmann's defense—that he was "just following orders"—could explain why his many accomplices, and the German people more broadly, went along with what they were told to do. Could this deference to authority explain why people acted contrary to their conscience?

Just three months after the Eichmann trial began, Milgram launched an experiment in which participants were instructed to perform an act that violated their conscience: the administration of a series of electric shocks upon a person in another room whom they could hear but not see. Each shock, participants were told, would be more powerful and painful than the last, leading to a final, fatal voltage being delivered. Of course, no pain was actually inflicted upon the unseen person, but participants did not know this and could only hear the unseen person's screams of agony. As participants protested throughout the process, they were instructed by the authority figure (an actor dressed in a lab coat) to continue—that the experiment was important and required completion. Reluctantly, most participants suppressed their concerns and did as instructed, to the point of (in their minds) administering death to another. Unlike many of the popular claims in psychology, the Milgram experiment has been consistently replicated, with results showing that over 60 percent of participants choose to inflict the fatal voltage upon the other person when instructed to do so by the authority figure.[32]

Sure, adults have a fully developed prefrontal cortex and can therefore make more rational, logical decisions. But despite this neurological advantage, adults easily fall prey to others—especially authority figures. There are at least two reasons why the human brain produces this result. The first is that it desires to conserve energy; around 20 percent of the body's energy usage is taken up by the brain, so it needs to be efficient.[33] And one way that the brain reduces its consumption is by looking for shortcuts—cues, patterns, and predictions that can expedite its decision-making. Consider this example: Last time you purchased something on Amazon.com, did you studiously review each of the photos, the description, features, specifications, and other product details? Chances are, the first thing you looked at was the rating—what its review average was and how many people had left a review. This social proof encourages us to copy the actions of others when choosing how we should behave. It's a shortcut; if thousands of people have taken the time to give a vacuum a high rating, you click the purchase button without spending much time reviewing details in depth. But taking shortcuts can be dangerous, especially when the masses are following the wrong leader. What seems popular, normal, or widely adopted may be completely absurd. Yet our brains want us to take the easy route and follow the crowd instead of doing our own thinking.

A second way adults fall prey to authority figures is the "amygdala hijack"—a process in the brain that overrides logical thinking due to an emotional response. Imagine an adult woman seeing a spider crawling on the floor near her foot. She jumps up in horror, climbing onto the nearby table. But why? This stimulus—the appearance of the spider—created a signal in her brain that was sent to the thalamus (the brain's "switchboard"), which routes data to different areas for processing. The thalamus split the signal into two, routing it both to the amygdala, which helps detect threats, and the neocortex, which handles sensory perception, reasoning, and conscious thought. When the spider stimulus hits the woman's brain, the amygdala quickly analyzes whether it matches an experience that she previously had. Perhaps as a young girl, she was nearly bitten by a black widow; this past experience would tell the brain that there is reason to fear, prompting her to jump onto the table. But what about the second signal, the one routed to the neocortex for rational thinking— to evaluate if the spider is *really* a threat? This path in the brain takes longer, meaning that the emotional response can beat out and override the rational one; if there's reason to fear, then the amygdala takes control and pushes rational thinking aside.[34] And that fear signal is especially powerful when the stimulus is a directive from an authority figure; the typical adult will fear being reprimanded, ostracized, punished, or even killed.

There are plenty of adult casualties in the mind war; young people have a disadvantage, to be sure, but world history offers countless examples of people of all ages falling prey to propaganda and doing what they were told—or what they see everyone else around them doing. It's tempting to "just follow orders" or follow the actions of the masses. And our brains encourage us to take the common path trod by others. But being vulnerable to the enemy's attack isn't a foregone conclusion; simply knowing how our brains make us vulnerable empowers us with knowledge to act differently. When we understand how the enemy exploits our emotions and uses psychology to manipulate us, we can weaponize that knowledge to resist.

HOW TO RESIST

On a brisk evening in 1983, famed magician David Copperfield stood before a seated audience on Liberty Island, home of the iconic Statue of Liberty. A helicopter circled overhead as spotlights illuminated the popular tourist attraction. Between two towers, Copperfield's team hoisted a large curtain to obstruct the audience's view of the statue. A nearby radar device showed its location... until suddenly, the green blip disappeared, suggesting the statue had mysteriously vanished! The curtain was lowered, and all the audience could see was the helicopter. Large searchlights probed the area, shining their light into an empty blackness where the statue had just moments ago stood. The audience—both those seated on the island and everyone watching at home—was mesmerized! "If I was home watching on TV, I would be a little skeptical," one of the people present said. "But I was here, and it was there... and now it's not there! I don't know what happened to it."[35] How could Copperfield have pulled off such a feat?

The secret involves a tool that magicians regularly employ: misdirection. This is a form of deception in which the performer draws the audience's attention to one thing in order to distract it from another. As the nineteenth-century magician Nevil Maskelyne put it, "It consists admittedly in misleading the spectator's senses, in order to screen from detection certain details for which secrecy is required."[36] And that's what Copperfield did. The audience happened to be seated on a rotating platform. As the curtain was raised, the misdirecting magician played loud music and distracted the audience with theatrics while the platform was slowly rotated just a few degrees. When the curtain was lowered, the view between the two towers showed nothing but the night sky, while the statue was now hidden behind one of the illuminated towers, making it very difficult to see. And Copperfield made sure no one looked closely enough to figure it out. The curtain was raised, the platform was rotated back to its original position, and the audience was left bewildered about how it had all been done.

Once you know, the illusion is dispelled. Those who felt mesmerized can quickly feel foolish, having been duped by something so basic. They realize that their attention was misdirected, and they were prevented from focusing on details that might have revealed the truth. As the saying goes, "Fool me once, shame on you; fool me twice, shame on me." Knowledge is power, and if we want to resist an enemy that wants to exploit our emotions and use psychology to manipulate and misdirect us, we need information; we need to understand things as they really are. But that's precisely what the propagandists, politicians, and pundits *don't* want. They don't want an informed citizenry of independent thinking, entrepreneurial individuals. They prefer that the masses live in deceptions that they can control. As one psychologist put it:

> Savvy propagandists... draw their power in
> large part from the fact that their targets are not
> aware that propaganda is being used on them.
> In this way, propaganda is not a magic show but
> a con. A mind that is not trained to detect and
> neutralize propaganda is a gullible mind, ripe
> for the swindle.[37]

The totalitarian regimes of history show the extreme versions of what we deal with daily: suppression
of information and thought control by an elite few. The
Nazis routinely burned books to suppress the unap-
proved ideas they contained and, once in power, elimi-
nated the freedom of the press. Any journalist critical
of Hitler and his Nazi allies faced prison or execution.
But the authoritarian hostility toward independent
ideas was certainly found elsewhere:

> Stalin, of course, was no more tolerant of criti-
> cism. Nor were Mao and Pol Pot. Pol Pot want-
> ed to eradicate not just the reality but even the
> memory of the old Capitalist Society, so he
> began by shifting the urban population to the
> country, away from books, newspapers, films
> and television. Then he began to "re-educate"
> them. Those who had been trained to think
> were most likely to be targeted. At least 1.5 mil-
> lion died.

Mao's "Cultural Revolution" similarly involved
the merciless eradication of all traces of un-
acceptable culture, which, unfortunately for
them, was rooted in the heads of his citizens.
Again, Mao focused on the educated, and particularly on educators. The result was the biggest killing spree in history.

What all three of these atheist mass-murderers—Stalin, Mao and Pol Pot—have in common
with the mass-murderers of the Holy Inquisi-
tion is an obsession with *controlling thought*. In
all three cases, we find Authoritarian regimes
slaughtering their own citizens *largely because
of the thoughts it was suspected those citizens
harbored in their heads*. It was, above all, those
who were, or were suspected of being, Enlightened, in Kant's sense of the term—those who
dared to think and question Authority—who
were exterminated like pests. The Twentieth
Century saw not only a Jewish Holocaust, but a
holocaust of the Enlightened.[38]

The masses' untrained minds are "ripe for the
swindle" and defer to authority, overriding even their
own contrarian consciences. How, then, can we resist?
What tactics can we employ to protect ourselves from
these societal patterns and thwart the enemy? While
the next chapter will focus on how we can go on the

offense, let's first explore a few ways that we can defensively shield our minds in order to not be deceived.

1. Cultivate Critical Thinking

Perhaps most obvious, and at the top of the list, is to develop a habit of critically evaluating information—especially when it comes from authoritative sources. Critical thinking is like a superpower for your brain, and it's something that can help you navigate the twists and turns of the modern world. Imagine being able to see through misleading ads, spot fake news, and make decisions based on facts rather than emotions. Start by questioning everything. Don't just accept things at face value; ask *why* and *how*. Turn it into a daily exercise; writing in a journal can be a great way to reflect on what's going on and think through your observations. Make it a practice to be curious and ask questions when presented with new information.

2. Stay Informed

If knowledge is power, then that's what you need. But first, you have to realize that much of the "news" that people rely on is manufactured and misleading. You need to sift through sources of information to identify credible organizations and individuals who deserve your trust. To do this, look for instances when journalists or individuals were willing to challenge their own "tribe"—for example, a progressive journalist who writes unflattering articles about the Democrats even though he leans "left" and is generally aligned with the Democratic party's goals and actions. Seeing people stand up to their own preferred group is a good sign that the person has integrity and principles. But we should still be skeptical even of these tentatively trusted people; you need to be ever on guard, cautiously curious about the information you're presented with. Always ask questions: Who benefits from this? How might this be biased? Is there another source that can corroborate what's reported here? Is more information needed before forming an opinion?

3. Be Skeptical of Authority

In a hierarchical society, we are surrounded by people in positions of influence or of power over us: elected officials, organizational leaders, influencers, doctors, church leaders, parents, coaches, and more. When a person in authority is telling us something, we need to resist believing it's true simply because of its "authoritative" source. Not everything a parent tells a child is actually accurate; and not everything a doctor claims is true. All of these people are fallible humans with their own biases and brain weaknesses that condition them to think, believe, and say things that may not be fully truthful. If our focus is truth, we need to be willing to challenge information that might not be correct, even if it comes from a source that we generally consider trustworthy and credible.

4. Balance Your Emotions

John Adams was one of the Founding Fathers intimately involved in helping craft the Constitution, including the First Amendment that says, "Congress shall make no law... abridging the freedom of speech." And yet, as president a decade later, Adams succumbed to fear about the French Revolution's potential effects on the new nation, so he signed into law the Sedition Act, which made it a crime to criticize the president or Congress! In too many instances, people who are afraid of something surrender their freedoms—or tolerate them being violated—because they feel that they need to be kept safe. (It's the reason why the TSA was created, for example.) Knowing about the "amygdala hijack," you can defend yourself by being more aware of your emotions and balancing them, so they do not lead you to take actions or believe things that are irrational or wrong.

5. Avoid Groupthink

In September 1973, Israel noticed Arab troop movements, but officials all believed that they didn't pose a threat. A month later, the Arabs attacked, and, in the ensuing conflict, thousands of soldiers on both sides of the battle died. It caught Israeli leadership off guard, so they made a policy change for future deliberations: the Tenth Man Rule. If nine people in a group of ten all agree on a particular conclusion, then it is the job of the tenth person to disagree and highlight all potential issues with that conclusion. Essentially, he plays the role of devil's advocate, a term with origins in the sixteenth-century Catholic Church, which established the role of *Advocatus Diaboli* to present counterevidence of sainthood and find reasons why someone should not be declared a saint. Some of the worst dangers come when everyone around you believes the same. Be on guard for groupthink, and in cases where there is widespread agreement on something, be the Tenth Man and determine if what everyone believes is actually true.

WIN THE WAR

One of the most important lessons I observed from *The Matrix* is that Neo has to *unlearn* falsehoods before he can *learn* truth. He had been raised, like most other humans, in a fake world—a programmed reality scripted and controlled by machines. What he thought was real simply wasn't. His entire worldview and understanding of truth were called into question. Naturally, he struggled to navigate this transition and understand the true nature of the false reality to which he had been subjected.

In one scene, Neo spars with Morpheus, his new mentor, in a simulated dojo environment. Neo fights using his human limitations—slower speed and heavy breathing. Morpheus teaches Neo that his power and potential far exceed what he had been programmed to believe. "I'm trying to free your mind, Neo," he tells him.

In the next scene, Morpheus and Neo are transported to a new simulated environment—this one on the rooftop of a skyscraper. "You have to let it all go, Neo," Morpheus continues. "Fear, doubt, and disbelief. Free your mind." He then jumps across the street, from rooftop to rooftop, illustrating his power to operate in this digital reality when freed from his programmed restraints.

Morpheus, Neo, and all their allies who were unplugged from the controlled virtual reality had an enemy: the machines. It was they who pulled humanity's strings, controlling their thoughts and actions. They had to unlearn the Matrix's deceptions before learning the truth—and once empowered by the truth, how to fight the enemy. This is also your task: to unlearn deceptions, learn the truth, and then fight the enemy. You, too, must free your mind.

To win the mind war, you must unlearn falsehoods. The fact is, you've been lied to—and repeatedly. Our parents grew up in this same mind war, but it has accelerated in recent decades, fueled by technological developments, social media, and everyone having a propaganda device in their pocket that they use hours each day. We've learned deceptions from teachers and textbooks; they permeate entertainment, academia, medicine, and more. Let's consider a brief list of examples to understand what we're up against.

- **Abraham Lincoln's goal was not to free the slaves.** Countless people believe and argue that Lincoln was on a quest to emancipate the slaves, and he receives a lot of credit for doing so. But that was not his goal. Lincoln once wrote: "My paramount object in this struggle is to save the Union and is not either to save or to destroy slavery. If I could save the Union without freeing any slave I would do it, and if I could save it by freeing all the slaves I would do it; and if I could save it by freeing some and leaving others alone I would also do that. What I do about slavery, and the colored race, I do because I believe it helps to save the Union; and what I forbear, I forbear because I do not believe it would help to save the Union."[1] In fact, Lincoln said he had "no purpose to introduce political and social equality between the white and black races" and that the differences between these races would "probably forever forbid their living together upon the footing of perfect equality."[2] Lincoln's chief goal was to bring the southern states to heel, forcing them to remain in the Union and not succeed—and in succeeding through a massively bloody military conflict, he changed what was a voluntary union of independent states into a coerced relationship of subordinate states to a domineering federal government. The country has never been the same since.[3]

- **Fossil fuels do not make extreme weather events worse.** Whenever there are alarming weather events such as a high-powered hurricane, many "climate change" alarmists across academia, entertainment, and corporate media unitedly assert that the Earth's warming is triggering more of these events. They blame fossil fuels and the CO2 emitted by their use, suggesting that the mom in a minivan driving her kids to soccer practice bears partial blame for other moms losing their entire home in the path of a hurricane's destruction. But none of this is true. Deaths from extreme weather have actually decreased 98 percent over the last century![4] And this is in large part thanks to fossil fuels directly, which allow us to build machines that protect people from storms, extreme temperatures, and drought. While critics complain that fossil fuels are causing these extreme temperatures, the reality is that temperature increases are a smaller danger than ever "thanks to fossil fueled heating and [air conditioning]— plus the net-benefits of warming in a world where far more people die of cold than heat."[5]

- **Dropping nuclear bombs on Japan wasn't necessary.** In 1991, President George H.W. Bush repeated a claim that schoolchildren have been taught for decades: dropping nuclear bombs in Japan, which killed around two hundred thousand people, most of them civilians, "spared millions of American lives."[6] This astounding number—nearly four times the total of US dead in all theaters in the Second World War—was a flagrant fabrication designed to soothe the conscience of the American public. General Douglas MacArthur, commander of the force that was preparing to invade Japan, estimated that the assault would only result in 95,000 American casualties, a third of them deaths.[7] When General Dwight D. Eisenhower, who later became president, learned of the plan to use the bombs, he said that he had "grave misgivings, first on the basis of my belief that Japan was already defeated and that dropping the bomb was completely unnecessary, and second because I thought that our country should avoid shocking world opinion by the use of a weapon whose employment was, I thought, no longer mandatory as a measure to save American lives. It was my belief that Japan was, at that very moment, seeking some way to surrender with a minimum loss of 'face.'"[8] He was right: Japanese leaders, both military and civilian, including the emperor, had been floating the idea of surrender for months, so long as the emperor—seen by the Japanese as a descendant of their god—could remain in place and not be subjected to war crimes. But President Roosevelt and then Truman afterward maintained a policy of unconditional surrender; they would not accept these terms and thus killed hundreds of thousands of people. Ironically, after the war concluded, the emperor was excluded from the tribunal to charge Japanese leaders with war crimes and was allowed to stay in power—the very conditions the United States had previously rejected in the march toward dropping the bombs. Of course, history is written by the victors, so US propagandists, politicians, and pundits shaped the narrative to justify the use of these bombs in what one former diplomat called an act of "fiendish butchery."[9]

There are abundant examples like these—things we were once taught to be true that in fact aren't. And they range from the serious, as in the examples above, to the more mundane—such as the false claims that we only use 10 percent of our brain, that chewing gum takes years to digest, or that goldfish have seconds-long attention spans. To win the mind war, we must understand things as they really are and root out any deceptions we have clung to. We must defensively resist the enemy's attacks, as outlined in the last chapter, by cultivating critical thinking, staying informed, being skeptical of authority, balancing our emotions, and avoiding groupthink. By developing these skills to learn truth and free our mind, we are ready to go on the offense to fight the enemy.

STAND UP

August Landmesser was born in 1910 in Moorrege, Germany, and was an only child. At age 21, seeking employment opportunities, he joined the Nazi Party. Four years later, he proposed to his girlfriend, Irma Eckler, a Jew. As a result, Landmesser was expelled from the Nazi Party. Undeterred, he went to nearby Hamburg to register his upcoming marriage, which was prohibited weeks later by the newly enacted Nuremberg Laws, which forbade marriage between Germans and Jews. Later that year, their first child was born—a girl named Ingrid.

Soon afterward, in 1936, Landmesser attended a gathering at the local shipyard with the other workers where a new navy ship was first launching. When prompted by the person conducting, everyone in the audience showed their support of *Der Führer* by extending their right arm to show their very best "Sieg Heil." But not Landmesser. He stood strong, defiant, grimacing as he kept both arms crossed over his chest while everyone around him obediently saluted.[10] Perhaps he was thinking of Irma, who, along with other Jews, was being systematically dehumanized by Hitler and his regime. Whatever was on his mind, his action was a clear result of independent thinking.

August Landmesser, refusing to salute

When student demonstrations erupted in the spring of 1989 in China, the Communist regime responded with a heavy military force. Automatic rifles and tanks were used to kill hundreds of unarmed civilians—and injure thousands—who were attempting to halt the military's advance towards Tiananmen Square, which demonstrators had occupied for several weeks. One man, whose identity remains unknown, placed himself at the front of a column of approaching tanks, repeatedly obstructing the lead tank as it attempted to maneuver around him.[11] Finally, two individuals pulled the man away, disappearing with him into a nearby crowd. For a brief moment in time, thankfully captured by a nearby videographer, this man defiantly stood up against tyranny.

Tanks rolling through Tiananmen Square; the protesting man is seen at bottom left in front of the first tank

History offers us a number of captivating stories, such as these where people stood up in a sit-down world, daring to stand firm in their convictions while everyone else mindlessly followed whatever the authority figures of the day demanded. We all celebrate those in history who refused to be controlled by powerful propaganda, yet many criticize such independent thinkers in the present day. Brutal wars and repressive regimes sometimes produce remarkable stories like these, where the stakes are high and those standing up against tyranny are so rare.

But standing up for truth in a mind war can (and should) happen far more commonly in these rare situations. It might mean stating that there are two genders when peers argue that there are dozens or that two-parent households are the best way to rear children when others contend that you're clinging to a patriarchal system of white supremacy. Maybe it involves arguing that taxation is theft when your neighbors are voting to increase your property taxes. Perhaps you defiantly bear multiple children in a world where people increasingly believe that humans cause climate change and that the population should be reduced. Standing up against deception and disinformation is something that can happen in your daily life; as you learn truth, you have an obligation to defend it—even if you stand alone.

If kids can do it, so can you. Twelve-year-old Jaiden Rodriguez was presented with his own opportunity to stand up on August 28, 2023, at the charter school he attended in Colorado Springs, Colorado. A longtime Tuttle Twins reader, young Jaiden was a passionately patriotic young man who had a number of patches on his backpack demonstrating his beliefs. One of them, a patch of the yellow "Don't tread on me" Gadsden flag, caught the attention of one of his teachers, who anonymously filed a complaint with the school administration. Jaiden was soon removed from class and was told that he could not return until he removed the patch, which they argued had "origins in slavery" and was "disruptive to the classroom environment."[12] Jaiden knew that these people were flat out wrong— that the Gadsden flag was an anti-British flag promoting colonial sovereignty in America and had

nothing to do with slavery whatsoever. So he refused to take the patch off and was removed from school. Within twenty-four hours, the school reversed course under immense pressure, as the story of Jaiden standing up for free

Jaiden, facing the disapproving look of the vice principal

speech and true American history went viral online.[13] It can be a scary thing for a twelve-year-old to stand up to adults, but Jaiden knew the truth. He was well-read and well-versed in what the Gadsden flag meant. Confident in his knowledge, he therefore had more confidence in his actions. He knew he was in the right and hoped he would be vindicated. History favors those, like him, who were on the right side of truth despite being surrounded with ignorance and bombarded with deceptions.

Jaiden's story has a positive outcome. He was able to return to class with the patch still displayed, and the school administrators were humbled once their ignorance and incorrectness were revealed. Millions of people learned about the Gadsden flag as well as American history and liberties, and Jaiden was given a platform to share his story in interviews, on podcasts, and with speaking engagements. Unfortunately, positive outcomes like this are not guaranteed. Quite often, in fact, those who stand up for truth are quickly shot down. Take Landmesser's story—he was imprisoned for "dishonoring the race" for loving a Jewish woman, arrested again, and sentenced to hard labor for nearly three years while his wife was snatched up by the Gestapo and ultimately executed in the gas chambers at Bernburg in 1942.[14]

To win the mind war, the enemy must maintain a particular narrative that reinforces its power—and that's why propaganda is an essential tool for its success. These Chinese Communists clearly opposed and suppressed the protests at Tiananmen Square, but the graver threat to their power was what these protests represented and their potential to embolden others to follow suit. So, the Chinese began censoring any mention of "Tank Man" and the protests. Their massive surveillance apparatus and firewall filtered out any mention on the internet, and authorities swiftly punished anyone attempting to publish stories about it. On the thirtieth anniversary of the protests in 2019, media across the world published stories remembering the events; none were accessible to those living in China. *The Global Times*, a state-run newspaper in China, did publish its own story that day saying that the massacre of hundreds of people thirty years earlier had been a "vaccination" against future "political turmoil," echoing the words of Defense Minister Wei Fenghe who said that the protests were "political turmoil that the central government needed to quell."[15]

Standing up in a mind war draws attention to you, just as Landmesser's refusal to salute was immediately apparent to others. In Aleksandr Solzhenitsyn's case, he was forcibly exiled by the Soviets for his anti-Com-

munist dissident views after he previously had been
sentenced to eight years in the Gulag for criticizing Joseph Stalin in a private letter.[16] But what finally set the
Soviets over the edge, leading them to expel Solzhenitsyn to the West, was the publication of his book *Gulag
Archipelago* in 1973, which exposed the vastness of the
secretive Gulag system, the repressive tactics used by
Soviet leaders, and the rotten Communist ideology that
produced this system. The night before fleeing Russia,
Solzhenitsyn published a final message to his country-
men titled "Live Not by Lies!" It was a powerful call to
action—a plea for others to stand up for truth:

> And it is not every day and not on every shoul-
> der that violence brings down its heavy hand: It
> demands of us only a submission to lies, a daily
> participation in deceit—and this suffices as our
> fealty.

> And therein we find, neglected by us, the sim-
> plest, the most accessible key to our liberation:
> a *personal nonparticipation in lies!* Even if all is
> covered by lies, even if all is under their rule, let
> us resist in the smallest way: Let their rule hold
> *not through me!*

> And this is the way to break out of the imagi-
> nary encirclement of our inertness, the easi-

est way for us and the most devastating for the lies. For when people renounce lies, lies simply cease to exist. Like parasites, they can only survive when attached to a person.

We are not called upon to step out onto the square and shout out the truth, to say out loud what we think—this is scary, we are not ready. But let us at least refuse to say what we *do not* think!

This is the way, then, the easiest and most accessible for us given our deep-seated organic cowardice, much easier than (it's scary even to utter the words) civil disobedience à la Gandhi.

Our way must be: *Never knowingly support lies!* Having understood where the lies begin (and many see this line differently)—step back from that gangrenous edge! Let us not glue back the flaking scales of the Ideology, not gather back its crumbling bones, nor patch together its decomposing garb, and we will be amazed how swiftly and helplessly the lies will fall away, and that which is destined to be naked will be exposed as such to the world.

And thus, overcoming our temerity, let each man choose: Will he remain a witting servant of the lies (needless to say, not due to natural predisposition, but in order to provide a living for the family, to rear the children in the spirit of lies!), or has the time come for him to stand straight as an honest man, worthy of the respect of his children and contemporaries?[17]

Powerful words. And we should heed Solzhenitsyn's counsel, for we are constantly encouraged to live by lies—to believe and repeat things that simply are not true. In today's mind war, objective truth itself has become a victim under assault from subjective moralists who preach that everyone should "speak your truth." This approach lets everyone be their own interpreter and judge, letting opinions and perceptions masquerade as something more. Suddenly we are expected to believe that men can have periods and become a "birthing person";[18] that equality demands treating people unequally;[19] that abortion is health care;[20] that words and thoughts are violence;[21] that natural immunity to diseases like COVID-19 doesn't exist;[22] and that saying two plus two equals four "reeks of white supremacist patriarchy."[23]

That last one is particularly amusing in light of its mention in George Orwell's *1984*. The novel's protagonist, Winston Smith, is being re-educated by the book's chief antagonist, O'Brien, a member of the Inner Party.

Winston is being tortured and subjected to demands
for intellectual obedience, to the point that his grip on
reality nears a breaking point. O'Brien holds up four
fingers, which Winston confirms. But if the Party says
that it's actually five, what then, wonders O'Brien
aloud? Winston responds that it would still be four.

> "You are a slow learner, Winston," said O'Brien
> gently.

> "How can I help it?" he blubbered. "How can
> I help seeing what is in front of my eyes? Two
> and two are four."

> "Sometimes, Winston. Sometimes they are five.
> Sometimes they are three. Sometimes they are
> all of them at once. You must try harder. It is
> not easy to become sane."[24]

Where Neo had to unlearn falsehood to learn truth,
Winston was forced to unlearn truth to learn falsehood. The reality was denied by the Party's philosophy, and when they decreed that two and two made
five, everyone was compelled to agree.

> The Party told you to reject the evidence of
> your eyes and ears. It was their final, most es-
> sential command. [Winston's] heart sank as he
> thought of the enormous power arrayed against

him, the ease with which any Party intellectual
would overthrow him in debate, the subtle arguments which he would not be able to understand, much less answer. And yet he was in the
right! They were wrong and he was right. The
obvious, the silly, and the true had got to be defended. Truisms are true, hold on to that! The
solid world exists, its laws do not change. Stones
are hard, water is wet, objects unsupported fall
towards the earth's centre. With the feeling that
he was speaking to O'Brien, and also that he
was setting forth an important axiom, he wrote:

Freedom is the freedom to say that two plus two
make four. If that is granted, all else follows.[25]

Today, the enemy tells you to reject the evidence
of your eyes and ears—to live by lies and repeat them
obediently to others. They are interested not in truth
but in compliance. Independent thinking is a threat to
their narrative. The enemy is vulnerable to the truth,
like the emperor without clothes, whose obvious na-
kedness is ignored by everyone who deluded themselves into ignoring this fact until a child stood apart
from the foolish members of the community and spoke
out. There does exist an objective reality, and all the deceptions and misdirection and propaganda—and soon,
AI-created deepfakes—in the world cannot change that

fact. Two plus two is, in fact, four. And truths such as this will remain true even if they are recognized only by a minority—and even if they are recognized only by you.

As terrifying as it may be to stand up for the truth, it's not enough; winning the mind war requires us to recruit others to the rebellion. Just as Morpheus and his crew liberated Neo and others to aid in the fight, we need to enlist others to join us. After all, standing up to a powerful army is far easier when we have allies by our side; there is strength in numbers. In the battle for truth, the more voices we have, the louder our message becomes and the closer we get to victory.

SPEAK OUT

Robert Scholl was a German father and an accountant by trade. Born in 1891, he and his wife, Magdalena, had six children together. Robert became a mayor in 1917 and served until 1930. He was a free thinker in his own right and a pacifist, having refused to serve in the military during World War I.[26] He had grave concerns about the rise of the Nazi Party and told colleagues in his office during the summer of 1942 that Hitler was a "divine scourge."[27] An employee denounced Robert and reported him to Gestapo officers, who arrived at the Scholls' home in Ulm the next morning to search the apartment and arrest Robert. At trial weeks later, he was sentenced to four months of imprisonment for "treachery." He had stood up for the truth—Hitler was indeed a scourge—and was consequently singled out and punished, as sometimes happens to those who act independently in ways the enemy disfavors.

It was two of his children, Hans and Sophie, who decided that standing up privately wasn't enough. They became determined to speak out.

Years of negative interactions had disillusioned both of them regarding the Nazi Party—activities that certainly added to the influence they felt from their father and his own views. But it wasn't always that way. Both had been members of the Hitler Youth, much to their father's chagrin, and Hans often argued with him about it. Sophie, at age twelve, wondered aloud why her Jewish friend wasn't allowed to join her in the organization.[28] As time went on, Hans started to detest the Nazis, and Sophie's views likewise changed. At age sixteen, she was arrested by the Gestapo after Hans was found to be a member of an anti-Hitler Youth group called Deutsche Jungenschaft. Sophie was released later that day, and Hans spent three weeks in prison, subjected to intense questioning. This experience helped solidify Sophie's anti-Nazi convictions and deepened her disinterest in her schoolwork that she felt had mostly become Nazi indoctrination.

Given her lack of interest in school, Sophie was barely accepted into the University of Munich in the fall of 1942, where Hans studied. Six weeks into her own studies, Sophie found a leaflet under a desk that bore the name White Rose. The words she read electrified her, giving voice to her own thoughts that she was still formulating in her mind; it had been only a few weeks since her father was sentenced to prison for his political views. The leaflet was a call to action—a warning cry about the unspeakable horrors being carried out by the Nazis. But something caught her attention: a sentence in the leaflet that exactly mirrored a passage from a philosophy book that Hans had read and underlined. She knew instantly that Hans was involved, and when she later confronted him about it, he reluctantly acknowledged his involvement after first denying it. "These days it is better not to know some things in case you endanger other people," he explained.[29] By the end of the conversation, Hans had told her everything about his resistance activities and had given her permission to join.

One member of the group later remarked that while Hans and a friend were the brains of the White Rose group, Sophie became its heart. She helped copy and distribute leaflets while preserving their anonymity—since this treasonous activity could get them killed. But

Sophie, like her elder brother, was passionate about speaking out to fellow Germans about what was really happening—what everyone knew was true but few would admit or openly discuss. "Why is the German nation behaving so apathetically in the face of all these most abominable, most degrading crimes?"[30] their second leaflet asked.

> Hardly anyone even gives them a second thought. The facts are accepted as just that and filed away. And one more time, the German nation slumbers on in its indifferent and foolish sleep and gives these fascist criminals courage and opportunity to rage on—which of course they do.

> Each man wishes to be acquitted of his complicity—everyone does so, then lies back down to sleep with a calm, clear conscience. But he may not acquit himself. Everyone is *guilty, guilty, guilty!*

> But it is not too late to rid the world of this most awful of all miscarriages of government, in order to avoid incurring even more guilt. Those of us who have had our eyes completely opened in recent years since we know with whom we are dealing—it is high time for us to exterminate this brown horde.[31]

Leaflets like this, with their provocative tones intended to stir people's hearts to action, were left in public phone booths, mailed to professors and students, and delivered to other universities. Thousands of copies were produced using a hand-operated duplicating machine and sent to cities throughout Germany. The fifth leaflet, written in January 1943, urged Germans to "Support the resistance movement!" in the struggle for "freedom of speech, freedom of religion, [and] the protection of the individual citizen from the caprice of criminal, violent States."[32] And their sixth, the last, announced a "day of reckoning" for "the most abominable tyrant that our nation has ever endured."[33]

A few weeks later, the Scholls carried a suitcase of their leaflets to the main building of the University of Munich. While students were inside their classrooms, Hans and Sophie dropped stacks of leaflets in the hallways, where the students would soon find and read them. Just as classes were getting out, Sophie pushed a stack of leaflets from the top floor banister over into the open atrium, which was noticed by a maintenance worker who called the Gestapo. The university doors were locked, and Hans and Sophie were soon taken into custody. Following heavy interrogation, both of the Scholls were sent for trial before the *Volksgerichtshof*—the Nazi "People's Court" known for its unfair political trials. As the judges talked, Sophie interrupted them: "Somebody had to make a start! What we said and wrote are what many people are thinking. They just don't dare say it out loud!" Four days after their arrest and on the same day of their trial, Hans and Sophie were executed by guillotine.

Recall that Solzhenitsyn wrote, "We are not called upon to step out onto the square and shout out the truth, to say out loud what we think—this is scary, we are not ready."[34] He said this with good reason; in the face of authoritarian regimes like the Soviets or the Nazis, speaking out is a careful calculus with many life-threatening variables. For him, it led to exile; for Hans and Sophie, it led to their death.

But sometimes we *are* called upon to shout out the truth—to wake up the world for the conflict of justice. This is especially true since so few among us realize the nature of the conflict itself; most people don't realize the mind war even exists, let alone who the enemy is and how it operates. Just prior to her execution, Sophie spoke some final remarks to her cellmate that should sting the conscience of any who feel like not speaking the truth widely to others. "How can we expect righteousness to prevail when there is hardly anyone willing to give himself up individually to a righteous cause? Such a fine, sunny day, and I have to go, but what does my death matter, if through us, thousands of people are awakened and stirred to action?"[35]

Thankfully, it is extremely rare for speaking out to incur a fatal consequence. You don't face the same risk that Sophie and Hans did. Your greatest threats are likely social shunning and "cancel culture"—being ostracized by others for your contrarian views. People will say mean things to you, assaulting you with *ad hominem* arguments since they often cannot debate the substance of their flawed ideas. They might attack your family members, colleagues, and friends. They might file a complaint with your employer or leave a negative review online about your business. Whatever the cost, this simple truth exists: those who learn the truth have an obligation to spread it.

Of course, truth is treason in an empire of lies. And if you're the sole person speaking out, you have reason to worry. It's one reason why John Locke published his *Two Treatises of Government* anonymously in 1689, concealing his identity not just from readers, but even his close friends and the publisher.[36] The book outlined what a civilized society should look like based on the protection of natural rights (the truth) and contrasted it against the absurd "divine right of kings" in support of a monarchy (the empire of lies) that Locke argued was "inconsistent with civil society":

...remember, that absolute monarchs are but men; and if government is to be the remedy of [the inconveniences of the state of nature]... I desire to know what kind of government that is, and how much better it is than the state of nature, where one man, commanding a multitude, has the liberty to be judge in his own case, and may do to all his subjects whatever he pleases, without the least liberty to any one to question or control those who execute his pleasure?[37]

Naturally, views like this would be unfavorable to a king who asserted to have divine backing for his authority. And because he was speaking out as one person, Locke rightly recognized that he might incur some form of backlash—being socially ostracized, prosecuted, or worse. When you're the only one speaking out against an empire of laws, you probably won't be speaking out for very long. Julian Assange from WikiLeaks would agree; after publishing evidence of war crimes committed by the US government in Iraq, Assange was indicted for espionage by that same government, which, at the time of writing, is attempting to extradite him to the country so he can languish in a maximum security prison.

When speaking out, it's often better to have friends; there is strength in numbers. It's why, when a group of freedom-minded statesmen penned their treasonous Declaration of Independence to the world's biggest superpower, they wrote, "We mutually pledge to each other our Lives, our Fortunes and our sacred Honor." It was a joint effort, signed by fifty-six delegates from thirteen colonies. A nearby printer stayed up all night printing around 200 copies for distribution; within days, the document was read to numerous audiences and reprinted in newspapers throughout the several states.[38] Hoping to inspire his troops, General George Washington read the document to his troops as thousands of British soldiers approached on ships.[39] Inflamed by the message, many in the crowd rushed to a nearby park where a statue of King George III had recently been placed. The 4,000-pound, lead statue was torn down and its head cut off; the metal was then melted down to produce tens of thousands of musket balls that would be used against the enemy.[40]

When these Founding Fathers spoke out, they did so surrounded by many supporters; the fact that there were many signers to the Declaration and many allies ready to further spread the message increased their odds and allowed them to successfully take on the enemy. Their physical war had literal strength in numbers; our psychological war can benefit from the same. This can come in a variety of forms. Here are a few simple examples:

- **Host a book club.** Create a reading group with friends, neighbors, or other peers where you read books that challenge the status quo. Dystopian fiction is a fun choice since it clearly shows what happens when the enemy is winning the mind war, but for nonfiction, you can choose books that disrupt conventional thinking and present alternative perspectives in order to try to better understand what's actually true. Focus on meaningful conversation to help others in your book club deepen their understanding and join you in brainstorming ways you can act upon the knowledge you're learning—how you can share it with others to speak out.

- **Organize cottage meetings.** Arrange small gatherings with friends or neighbors to hear from people in your community—an elected official, a reporter, or other community leader. They'll appreciate the opportunity to present their message to a group; they'll see you as a "connector" worth getting to know; and your group will have an opportunity to ask challenging questions about pressing issues.

- **Crowdfund a controversial billboard.** Raise some money with friends to put up a billboard in a prominent place in your community, featuring a message that boldly tells the truth about an issue you feel passionate about. It could be about inflation and the economy, war, the pharmaceutical industry, abortion, the police, free speech, or any number of issues. If the message is powerful, the local media will often do a story about the billboard, helping your message to be seen by even more people.

- **Start a podcast or YouTube channel.** Join up with some like-minded friends to discuss current events or recent trends, so you can broadcast your thoughts and views to a wider audience and build a community of people who can learn from what you have to share. Become known as a truth teller and attract others who are curious about learning truth.

- **Become a propagandist.** Ultimately, propaganda is the propagation of an idea—spreading a message. While the enemy does it with their falsehoods, you can also do it to promote truth. For example, in promoting ratification of the Constitution, a few Founding Fathers began writing essays under the pseudonym Publius, advocating for this new proposal—they kept their identities a secret to focus attention on the

message. You can team up with some friends to
start an online newsletter, an email list, a social
media account, or other form of communication to boldly speak out about truths using a
pen name that masks your identity.

At the 2009 Sasquatch Music Festival in Seattle,
Washington, concertgoers were spread out across an
open lawn, sitting on blankets to listen to the various
bands play. One man defied the norm and stood to begin dancing. It was clearly awkward; someone pulled
out their phone to record the oddball dancing without
an apparent care in the world. Arms and legs flailing
around, he acted out what he thought was right for the
occasion, despite everyone else around him evident-
ly disagreeing. That is, until one other person stood
up. That second individual joined the first to dance,
and for thirty-five seconds, the two of them bounced
around exuberantly. Then a third stood up. Twenty
seconds later, two others approached to join in the fun.
Four seconds later, three more began dancing too. For
several seconds, one or two people began joining the
group, until soon it became a steady stream of people,
quickly expanding the size of the crowd. In short order, nearly the entire crowd was on their feet in a riot-
ous act of self-expression.[41] Sometimes all it takes is
one person to influence the masses.

But you might feel reluctant in speaking out because you feel that your sphere of influence is small. Is it worth all the effort to stand up and broadcast the truth to others if only a few will listen? The reality of the Sasquatch story is that the masses would not have been influenced like they were without the *second* person's involvement. It was that decision to turn a single act of standing up into a (small) group of people acting out that began the trickle that became the flood. The first guy really only influenced one other person, but *that was enough*. The second guy influenced a third, whose action influenced a fourth, and so on. Sometimes our sphere of influence is small, but there is still power in speaking out to a tiny audience. That might only be members of your own family. But that might be enough. When Jaiden stood up to his ignorant school administrators over their insanely wrong views of American history, it was because of his mother's influence and teachings—one person speaking out to another. Robert Scholl spoke out to colleagues, but that message didn't spread—it was speaking out to his own children that had the effect of educating millions of people through their own efforts. Sometimes this form of speaking out—to the few people we can influence the most—is the most important.

CONCLUSION

In a mind war, many of the strategies shared in Sun Tzu's *The Art of War* appear to be relevant and helpful. "Those skilled in warfare move the enemy, and are not moved *by* the enemy," reads one.[1] Instead of playing defense, we need to be far better about uniting together to go on the offensive and limit the power of propagandists, politicians, and pundits. Another strategy says, "If our army is at full force and the enemy is divided, then we will attack him at ten times his strength."[2] The side with unified strength has leverage over the confused, divided opponent; united we stand, divided we fall.

Maybe Sun Tzu had some linguistic inspiration in his strategies. In Chinese, the word for *crisis* is 危机. Note that there are two characters that form the word. The first character means danger; the second means opportunity. Thus, a crisis is seen in two lights: it can be dangerous, but there is also a silver lining—the opportunity that a crisis inevitably produces. Yes, we're in a mind war. Yes, there are very sophisticated and powerful people trying to exploit your emotions, influence your mind, and alter your actions. And yes, it can seem like an uphill (or impossible) battle at times. But this psychological crisis, despite its many dangers, brings with it an opportunity for truth tellers like you who want to win the war.

The very conditions that make this battle so daunting—the pervasive influence of social media, the degradation of shared truths, and the sheer volume of information overwhelming our senses on a daily basis—also create fertile ground for transformative change. Just as the crisis reveals our vulnerabilities, it also uncovers our strengths. It allows us—perhaps forces us—to question the foundations of our beliefs, reevaluate our sources of information, and scrutinize the intentions behind the messages we consume. Consider the crisis of truth that AI deepfakes and easily manipulated video content will produce. In a world awash with manipulated imagery, how can we tell what is true? With tools like these easily accessible to the masses, there will be an explosion of trickery permeating our social media feeds regularly. Yet, this deluge of deception presents an opportunity; if people are so overwhelmed with manipulated content, perhaps they can develop a strong skepticism of the information they are presented with. Perhaps they can enhance their critical thinking skills and regularly question what they see by default. Maybe innovative entrepreneurs, rising to the occasion, will develop new systems that allow us to certify authentic and true content in order to filter out the machine-generated noise. As people become more aware of the tactics used to manipulate them, they also grow more discerning, more critical, and ultimately more empowered. Amidst the dangers of the mind war, the opportunity arises for each of us to become not just consumers of information but also curators of truth. This is our silver lining, our chance to turn the tables and reclaim control over our own minds.

Recognize that this is not a battle to be fought and won alone. Just as in any war, there are roles for each of us to play, strategies to employ, and alliances to build. We won't have strength unless we have the numbers. And the collective power of many informed individuals, each standing up and speaking out, is the strongest weapon against the dark forces that seek to manipulate our minds; truth is treason in an empire of lies. Simply knowing that the battle is happening is the first step toward winning it. But our objective shouldn't be just to win battles; we need to secure a lasting peace—an intellectual and emotional peace based on the bedrock of truth. That peace starts with you—with the choices you make every day about what to learn and from which sources; what to share and with whom; and how well you fortify your mind to guard against its inherent weaknesses.

The time for complacency has ended. Each of us is a soldier, involuntarily drafted into this mind war, charged with defensively fortifying our minds and then gaining ground on the enemy. In times of universal deceit, speaking the truth is a revolutionary act. This is not passive behavior; it's a daily commitment to question, to seek, and above all, to share the light of truth in the dark corners of deception. You are no longer just an observer, but an active participant. See you on the battlefield!

INTRODUCTION

1. Nathan Bradley, "Bombs and the Boy," *McSweeney's*, October 19, 2011, https://www.mcsweeneys.net/articles/column-20-bombs-and-the-boy.
2. Ibid.
3. "How 775,000 U.S. troops fought in one war: Afghanistan military deployments by the numbers," *The Washington Post*, September 11, 2019, https://www.washingtonpost.com/national-security/2019/09/11/how-us-troops-fought-one-war-afghanistan-military-deployments-by-numbers/.
4. Sun Tzu, *The Art of War* (Norderstedt: Books on Demand, 2020), 23.
5. "Soldiers Expose Deployment of Unprepared Troops," CounterPunch, August 10, 2010, https://www.counterpunch.org/2010/08/10/soldiers-expose-deployment-of-unprepared-troops/.
6. Ibid.
7. "Up to 75 Percent of US Youth Ineligible for Military Service," ThoughtCo, September 2, 2021, https://www.thoughtco.com/us-youth-ineligible-for-military-service-3322428.

KNOW THY ENEMY

1. *The Matrix*, directed by Andy Wachowski and Larry Wachowski (Warner Bros. Pictures, 1999).
2. C.S. Lewis, "The Humanitarian Theory of Punishment," *Twentieth Century*, 228.
3. Peter Longerich, *Goebbels: A Biography* (New York: Random House, 2015), 16.
4. Ibid., 34.

5. Ibid., 37.
6. Joachim Fest, *The Face Of The Third Reich: Portraits Of The Nazi Leadership* (New York: Pantheon, 1970), 90.
7. Toby Thacker, *Joseph Goebbels: Life and Death* (New York: Palgrave Macmillan, 2009), 316.
8. Adolf Hitler, as quoted in *Trials of War Criminals Before the Nuremberg Military Tribunals, vol. 14* (Washington, D.C.: U.S. Government, 1949), 569.
9. Thacker, *Joseph Goebbels: Life and Death*, 316.
10. Ibid.
11. Bernays wrote in his autobiography, "They were using my books as the basis for a destructive campaign against the Jews of Germany. This shocked me, but I knew any human activity can be used for social purposes or misused for antisocial ones." See *Biography of an Idea: Memoirs of Public Relations Counsel* (New York: Simon and Schuster, 1965), 652.
12. Edward Bernays, "The Engineering of Consent," *The Annals of the American Academy*, https://web.archive.org/web/20120813014102/http://gromitinc.com/lego/Library/Engineering_of_consent.pdf.
13. Ibid.
14. Ibid.
15. Ibid.
16. David Pescovitz, "Case Sunstein: Feds should 'cognitively infiltrate' online conspiracy groups," BoingBoing, https://boingboing.net/2010/02/08/case-sunstein-feds-s.html.
17. Cass R. Sunstein and Adrian Vermeule, "Conspiracy Theories", *Harvard Public Law* Working Paper No. 08-03, University of Chicago, January 15,

2008, https://ssrn.com/abstract=1084585 or http://dx.doi.org/10.2139/ssrn.1084585.

18. Richard Thaler and Cass Sunstein, *Nudge: Improving Decisions About Health, Wealth, and Happiness* (New York: Penguin Group, 2008), 5.

19. Craig S. Neumann and Robert D. Hare, "Psychopathic Traits in a Large Community Sample: Links to Violence, Alcohol Use, and Intelligence," *Journal of Consulting and Clinical Psychology*, http://www.hare.org/references/Neumannand-HareJCCP2008.pdf.

20. "Psychopathy," Wikipedia, accessed February 1, 2023, https://en.wikipedia.org/wiki/Psychopathy.

21. "Almost Psychopaths Chronically Lie, Manipulate, but Fall Short of a Diagnosis," ABC News, June 18, 2012, https://abcnews.go.com/Health/psychopath-book-ids-subclinical-lying-manipulating-callous-behavior/story?id=16598607.

22. "Catapulting the Propaganda," Mother Jones, August 29, 2005, https://www.motherjones.com/politics/2005/08/catapulting-propaganda/.

23. Jonathan Turley, "WikiLeaks-founder Julian Assange will be punished for embarrassing the DC establishment," *The Herald-Mail*, April 11, 2019, https://www.heraldmailmedia.com/story/news/2019/04/11/wikileaks-founder-julian-assange-will-be-punished-for-embarrassing-the-dc-establishme/116437940/.

24. "Trump Is Not the First Republican to Campaign Against Nation-building," AEI, May 3, 2016, https://www.aei.org/foreign-and-defense-policy/middle-east/trump-is-not-the-first-republican-to-campaign-against-nation-building/.

25. "Bush's Betrayal of Free-Market Principles Now

Complete," The Daily Signal, December 30, 2008, https://www.dailysignal.com/2008/12/30/bushs-betrayal-of-free-market-principles-now-complete/.

26. "TaxVox: Campaigns, Proposals, and Reforms," Tax Policy Center, December 5, 2018, https://www.taxpolicycenter.org/taxvox/reading-president-bushs-lips.

27. Ibid.

28. "Obama: 'If you like your health care plan…,'" PolitiFact, accessed February 1, 2023, https://www.politifact.com/obama-like-health-care-keep/.

29. "Obama's 'You Can Keep It' Promise Is 'Lie Of The Year,'" NPR, December 13, 2013, https://www.npr.org/sections/thetwo-way/2013/12/13/250694372/obamas-you-can-keep-it-promise-is-lie-of-the-year.

30. "The 5 Broken Promises of Obamacare," Texas Public Policy Foundation, September 22, 2020, https://www.texaspolicy.com/brokenpromises/.

31. "How Franklin Roosevelt Lied America Into War," Institute for Historical Review, accessed February 11, 2023, http://www.ihr.org/jhr/v14/v14n6p19_Chamberlin.html.

32. Ibid.

33. See Robert B. Stinnett, *Day of Deceit: The Truth about FDR and Pearl Harbor* (New York: Touchstone, 2000).

34. "Joe Biden Sends Tanks to Ukraine After Warning Doing So Would Be 'World War III,'" Breitbart, January 31, 2023, https://www.breitbart.com/politics/2023/01/31/joe-biden-sends-tanks-to-ukraine-after-warning-doing-so-would-be-world-war-iii/.

35. "These 12 High-Profile Politicians Got Caught Violating Their Own COVID Rules," Foundation for Economic Education, August 2, 2021, https://fee.org/articles/these-12-high-profile-politicians-got-caught-violating-their-own-covid-rules/.
36. Ibid.
37. Ibid.
38. "Politics and the English Language," The Orwell Foundation, accessed February 11, 2023, https://www.orwellfoundation.com/the-orwell-foundation/orwell/essays-and-other-works/politics-and-the-english-language/.
39. Niccolò Machiavelli, *The Prince* (London: J.M. Dent & Sons, 1948), 106.
40. Ibid.
41. Ibid., 95.
42. "Lying politicians: A fact of life," CBS News, August 3, 2012, https://www.cbsnews.com/news/lying-politicians-a-fact-of-life/.
43. Humphrey Carpenter, ed., *The Letters of J.R.R. Tolkien* (London: George Allen & Unwin), 52.
44. Deborah Davis, *Katharine the Great: Katharine Graham and her Washington Post Empire* (Sheridan Square Press, Inc., 1991), 119.
45. Ibid.
46. "The CIA and the Media," Rolling Stone, October 20, 1977, https://www.carlbernstein.com/the-cia-and-the-media-rolling-stone-10-20-1977.
47. Loch K. Johnson, *America's Secret Power: The CIA in a Democratic Society* (Oxford: Oxford University Press, 1991), 186.
48. "When the CIA Interferes in Foreign Elections," *Foreign Affairs*, June 21, 2020, https://www.foreignaffairs.com/articles/united-states/2020-06-21/

cia-interferes-foreign-elections.

49. For example, former Joe Biden spokeswoman Jen Psaki was given a TV show called "Inside with Jen Psaki" on MSNBC. George Stephanopoulos, who hosts two shows on ABC, was Bill Clinton's communications director. Kayleigh McEnany, who started in the media, became Donald Trump's press secretary, and later a co-host of a Fox News show. Countless other examples exist.

50. "The Spies Who Came in to the TV Studio," *Politico Magazine*, February 6, 2018, https://www.politico.com/magazine/story/2018/02/06/john-brennan-james-claper-michael-hayden-former-cia-media-216943/.

51. "Behind TV Analysts, Pentagon's Hidden Hand," *The New York Times*, April 20, 2008, https://www.nytimes.com/2008/04/20/us/20generals.html.

52. Ibid.

53. "Griffin: Those are Soviet era bio-labs, Twitter, Acyn, March 9, 2022, https://twitter.com/Acyn/status/1501744772188307460.

54. "Trust in media is so low that half of Americans now believe that news organizations deliberately mislead them," Fortune, February 15, 2023, https://fortune.com/2023/02/15/trust-in-media-low-misinform-mislead-biased-republicans-democrats-poll-gallup/.

55. Ibid.

56. "Americans' Trust In Media Remains Near Record Low," Gallup, October 18, 2022, https://news.gallup.com/poll/403166/americans-trust-media-remains-near-record-low.aspx.

57. R. F. Christian, ed., *Tolstoy's Diaries, vol. 2* (London: Athlone Press, 1985), 512.

58. "Seymour Hersh on Obama, NSA and the 'pathetic' American media," *The Guardian*, September 27, 2013, http://www.theguardian.com/media/media-blog/2013/sep/27/seymour-hersh-obama-nsa-american-media.

59. "CBS Anchor: 'We Are Getting Big Stories Wrong, Over and Over Again,'" The Weekly Standard, May 11, 2013, http://www.weeklystandard.com/blogs/cbs-anchor-we-are-getting-big-stories-wrong-over-and-over-again_722331.html.

60. "The Career-Advancing Lies of Corporate Journalists," System Update, December 30, 2022, https://systemupdate.substack.com/p/the-career-advancing-lies-of-corporate.

61. "Source of CIA Director William J. Casey's Disinformation Program Quote," Archive.org, accessed February 26, 2023, https://archive.org/details/cia-director-william-casey-disinformation-program-quote-soruce.

62. Joyce Appleby and Terence Ball, *Jefferson: Political Writings* (Cambridge: Cambridge University Press, 1999), 275.

PROPAGANDA IS POWER

1. Actually, Edward was his double nephew. Edward's father, Ely, was the brother of Martha, Sigmund Freud's wife. And Edwards mother, Anna, was Sigmund Freud's sister, Anna.

2. Alan Axelrod, *Selling the Great War: The Making of American Propaganda* (Manhattan: St. Martin's Publishing Group, 2009), 200.

3. Scott Cutlip, *The Unseen Power: Public Relations. A History* (Hove: Lawrence Erlbaum, 1994), 168.

4. "Bacon, Eggs, and Public Relations: How PR Pioneer Edward L. Bernays Changed America," This is Capitalism, January 23, 2020, https://www.thisiscapitalism.com/bacon-eggs-and-public-relations/.

5. Edward Bernays, *Crystallizing Public Opinion* (New York: Liveright Publishing Co., 1923), 171.

6. Edward Bernays, *Propaganda* (Brooklyn: IG Publishing, 2005), 37.

7. Ibid., 38.

8. "The Secret History of the Shadow Campaign That Saved the 2020 Election," *TIME*, February 4, 2021, https://time.com/5936036/secret-2020-election-campaign/.

9. Much later in life, Bernays wrote a book called *The Engineering of Consent*, a term which he defined as "the application of scientific principles and tried practices to the task of getting people to support ideas and programs."

10. "Witnesses describe atrocities by Iraqis," The Commercial Appeal, October 11, 1990.

11. "Remember Nayirah, Witness for Kuwait?," *The New York Times*, January 6, 1992.

12. "How PR Sold the War in the Persian Gulf," PR Watch, accessed March 1, 2023, https://www.prwatch.org/books/tsigfy10.html.

13. "Operation Northwoods," Wikipedia, accessed March 1, 2023, https://en.wikipedia.org/wiki/Operation_Northwoods.

14. Ibid.

15. Lloyd Free and Hadley Cantril, *The Political Beliefs of Americans* (New York: Simon & Schuster, 1968), 59-60.

16. "The Truth About Tonkin," U.S. Naval Institute,

February 2008, https://www.usni.org/magazines/naval-history-magazine/2008/february/truth-about-tonkin.

17. "U.S. public opinion towards the involvement of U.S. ground forces in the Vietnam War from 1965 to 1973," Statista, accessed March 1, 2023, https://www.statista.com/statistics/1334328/vietnam-war-us-public-opinion-mistake/.

18. James Wirtz and Roy Godson, *Strategic Denial and Deception: The Twenty-First Century Challenge* (New Jersey: Transaction Publishers, 2002),100.

19. "John Bolton says he 'helped plan coups d'etat' in other countries," *The Guardian*, July 13, 2022, https://www.theguardian.com/us-news/2022/jul/13/john-bolton-planned-coups-donald-trump-january-6.

20. Charles A. Elmwood, "Making the World Safe for Democracy," *The Scientific Monthly*, vol. 7, no. 6 (Dec 1918), 511.

21. "Four Minute Men," Wikipedia, accessed March 19, 2023, https://en.wikipedia.org/wiki/Four_Minute_Men.

22. Ibid.

23. Ray L. Hall, "Seeing is Believing," *The Independent*, September 18, 1926.

24. Ibid.

25. *The Activities of the Committee on Public Information*, no. 18 (Government Printing Office: Washington, DC, 1918), 8.

26. Erick Van Schaack, "The Division of Pictorial Publicity in World War I," *Design Issues, vol. 22, no. 1* (2006), 44-45.

27. Harold Tobin and Percy Bidwell, *Mobilizing Civilian America* (Council on Foreign Relations, 1940),

75-76.

28. "Matt Taibbi rips Twitter, mainstream media over 'digital McCarthyism,'" *New York Post*, March 9, 2023, https://nypost.com/2023/03/09/matt-taibbi-eviscerates-twitter-in-congressional-hearing/.

29. "Google teams up with UN for verified climate information," United Nations, April 22, 2022, https://www.un.org/en/climatechange/google-search-information.

30. Ibid.

31. "SUPERCUT!," Tom Elliott, Twitter, October 15, 2021, https://twitter.com/tomselliott/status/1448986127545864199.

32. "Stanford's Dark Hand in Twitter Censorship," The Stanford Review, March 24, 2023, https://stanfordreview.org/stanfords-dark-hand-in-twitter-censorship/.

33. "Biden warns of winter of 'severe illness and death' for unvaccinated due to Omicron," CNN, December 16, 2021, https://www.cnn.com/2021/12/16/politics/joe-biden-warning-winter/index.html.

34. "A timeline of the CDC's advice on face masks," *Los Angeles Times*, July 27, 2021, https://www.latimes.com/science/story/2021-07-27/timeline-cdc-mask-guidance-during-covid-19-pandemic.

35. "The Mask Mandates Did Nothing. Will Any Lessons Be Learned?," *The New York Times*, February 21, 2013, https://www.nytimes.com/2023/02/21/opinion/do-mask-mandates-work.html.

36. Peter Van Buren, "COVID, Learned Helplessness, and Control," Medium, May 22, 2021, https://wemeantwell.medium.com/covid-learned-helplessness-and-control-a156823bd123.

37. "The Pfizer Vaccine Is 100 Percent Effective for

People This Age, Study Says," Yahoo, March 31, 2021, https://www.yahoo.com/lifestyle/pfizer-vaccine-100-percent-effective-133341287.html.

38. "Pfizer/BioNTech says its Covid-19 vaccine is 100% effective," CNN, March 31, 2021, https://www.cnn.com/2021/03/31/health/pfizer-vaccine-adolescent-trial-results/index.html.

39. "Pfizer vaccine 96.7% effective at preventing COVID deaths, Israeli data shows," The Times of Israel, May 6, 2021, https://www.timesofisrael.com/pfizer-vaccine-96-7-effective-at-preventing-covid-deaths-israeli-data-shows/.

40. "Study: Pfizer vaccine 88 percent effective against delta variant," The Hill, July 22, 2021, https://thehill.com/policy/healthcare/564288-study-pfizer-vaccine-88-percent-effective-against-delta-variant/.

41. "Health Ministry says COVID vaccine is only 40% effective at halting transmission," The Times of Israel, July 22, 2021, https://www.timesofisrael.com/liveblog_entry/health-ministry-says-covid-vaccine-is-only-40-effective-at-halting-transmission/.

42. "Moderna Covid vaccine 76% effective against Delta, Pfizer 42%: Study," Business standard, August 12, 2021, https://www.business-standard.com/article/current-affairs/moderna-covid-vaccine-76-effective-against-delta-pfizer-42-study-121081201173_1.html.

43. "Pfizer's Covid vaccine efficacy against infection plunges to just 20% after six months - but protection against severe illness barely dips, study concludes," The Daily Mail, October 7, 2021, https://www.dailymail.co.uk/news/article-10064291/Pfizers-Covid-efficacy-against-infection-plunges-

20-six-months-data-Qatar-shows.html.

44. "AP FACT CHECK: Biden goes too far in assurances on vaccines," AP News, July 21, 2021, https://apnews.com/article/joe-biden-business-health-government-and-politics-coronavirus-pandemic-46a270ce0f681caa7e4143e2ae9a0211.

45. "Can Vaccinated People Spread the Virus? We Don't Know, Scientists Say.," *The New York Times*, April 1, 2021, https://www.nytimes.com/2021/04/01/health/coronavirus-vaccine-walensky.html.

46. Viewers demand apology from MSNBC, Rachel Maddow for previous COVID vaccine comments," Fox News, December 28, 2021, https://www.foxnews.com/media/social-media-users-demand-apology-msnbc-rachel-maddow-vaccines.

47. "Federal Reserve calls inflation 'transitory' as it keeps interest rates near zero," CBS News, April 28, 2021, https://www.cbsnews.com/news/interest-rates-inflation-federal-reserve-transitory/.

48. "Inflation is hotter than expected, but it looks temporary and likely won't affect Fed policy yet," CNBC, June 10, 2021, https://www.cnbc.com/2021/06/10/inflation-hotter-than-expected-but-transitory-wont-affect-fed-policy.html.

49. "Fed Officials See 'Transitory' Inflation Lasting Quite a While," *The Wall Street Journal*, September 23, 2021, https://www.wsj.com/articles/fed-officials-see-transitory-inflation-lasting-quite-a-while-11632389401.

50. "U.S. inflation at 9.1 percent, a record high," PBS, July 13, 2022, https://www.pbs.org/newshour/economy/u-s-inflation-at-9-1-percent-a-record-high.

51. "Why inflation refuses to go away," The Economist, October 19, 2022, https://www.economist.com/finance-and-economics/2022/10/19/why-inflation-refuses-to-go-away.

52. "People need to accept they are poorer, says Bank of England," *The Telegraph*, April 26, 2023, https://www.msn.com/en-gb/money/other/people-need-to-accept-they-are-poorer-says-bank-of-england/ar-AA1ajSNY.

53. "When You Are Not With Where a Majority of Americans Are, Then, You Know, That Is Extreme," Reason, September 2, 2022, https://reason.com/volokh/2022/09/02/when-you-are-not-with-where-a-majority-of-americans-are-then-you-know-that-is-extreme/.

54. "Demonizing the Enemy a Hallmark of War," ABC News, January 29, 2003, https://abcnews.go.com/International/story?id=79071.

55. "A dead Iraqi is just another dead Iraqi... You know, so what?," *The Independent*, July 12, 2007, https://www.independent.co.uk/news/world/americas/a-dead-iraqi-is-just-another-dead-iraqi-you-know-so-what-5333968.html.

56. "US warns of new Falluja offensive," BBC, April 21, 2004, http://news.bbc.co.uk/2/hi/middle_east/3644565.stm.

57. "The NSA's Word Games Explained: How the Government Deceived Congress in the Debate over Surveillance Powers," Electronic Frontier Foundation, June 11, 2013, https://www.eff.org/deeplinks/2013/06/director-national-intelligences-word-games-explained-how-government-deceived.

58. "Tuskegee Syphilis Study," Wikipedia, accessed

May 20, 2023, https://en.wikipedia.org/wiki/Tuskegee_Syphilis_Study.

59. "NPR tells readers the Hunter Biden story is a 'waste' of time and a 'pure distraction,' so they're not reporting on it," The Blaze, October 22, 2020, https://www.theblaze.com/news/npr-hunter-biden-story-waste-distraction.

60. "The Hunter Biden Statement: How Senior Intelligence Community Officials and the Biden Campaign Worked to Mislead American Voters," Interim Joint Staff Report of the Committee on the Judiciary, May 10, 2023.

61. "Biden Weighs Mike Morell as His CIA Chief. A Key Dem Senator Says Don't Bother," The Daily Best, December 2, 2020, https://www.thedaily-beast.com/biden-weighs-mike-morell-as-his-cia-chief-a-key-dem-senator-says-dont-bother.

62. "To Fight Vaccine Lies, Authorities Recruit an 'Influencer Army,'" The New York Times, August 1, 2021, https://www.nytimes.com/2021/08/01/technology/vaccine-lies-influencer-army.html.

63. "Biden's digital strategy: an army of influencers," Axios, April 9, 2023, https://www.axios.com/2023/04/09/bidens-digital-strategy-an-army-of-influencers.

BEWARE THE EXPERTS

1. "Texas court throws out 1987 murder conviction; declares North Texas man "actually innocent"," The Texas Tribune, December 19, 2018, https://www.texastribune.org/2018/12/19/steven-mark-chaney-murder-conviction-overturned/.

2. Ibid.

3. "Jailed Texas man free after 28 years as bite evidence thrown out in murder case," *The Guardian*, October 12, 2015, https://www.theguardian.com/us-news/2015/oct/13/jailed-texas-man-free-after-28-years-as-bite-evidence-thrown-out-in-case.

4. "'We are going backward': How the justice system ignores science in the pursuit of convictions," NBC News, January 23, 2019, https://www.nbcnews.com/news/us-news/we-are-going-backward-how-justice-system-ignores-science-pursuit-n961256.

5. "Americans' Trust In Media Remains Near Record Low," Gallup, October 18, 2022, https://news.gallup.com/poll/403166/americans-trust-media-remains-near-record-low.aspx.

6. "Just 26% of Americans…," Michael Shellenberger, Twitter, February 17, 2023, https://twitter.com/shellenberger/status/1626586691720060929.

7. "American Views 2022: Part 2," Knight Foundation, January 2023, https://knightfoundation.org/wp-content/uploads/2023/02/American-Views-2022-Pt-2-Trust-Media-and-Democracy.pdf.

8. Ibid.

9. "Saddam Hussein and the Sept. 11 Attacks," *Washington Post*, September 6, 2003, https://www.washingtonpost.com/wp-srv/politics/polls/vault/stories/data082303.htm.

10. "Harvard professor who studies honesty accused of falsifying data in studies," *The Guardian*, June 25, 2023, https://www.theguardian.com/education/2023/jun/25/harvard-professor-data-fraud.

11. "Fauci: Attacks on me are really also 'attacks on science'," The Hill, June 9, 2021, https://thehill.com/policy/healthcare/557602-fauci-attacks-on-

me-are-really-also-attacks-on-science/.

12. "MSNBC's Brzezinski: Trump Thinks He Can 'Control Exactly What People Think,' But That's 'Our Job,'" RealClearPolitics, February 22, 2017, https://www.realclearpolitics.com/video/2017/02/22/msnbcs_brzezinski_trump_thinks_he_can_control_exactly_what_people_think_but_thats_our_job.html

13. "Casualties of the Iraq War," Wikipedia, accessed July 12, 2023, https://en.wikipedia.org/wiki/Casualties_of_the_Iraq_War.

14. "Financial cost of the Iraq War," Wikipedia, accessed July 12, 2023, https://en.wikipedia.org/wiki/Financial_cost_of_the_Iraq_War.

15. "Iraq war, 20 years on: how the world failed Iraq and created a less peaceful, democratic and prosperous state," The Conversation, March 16, 2023, https://theconversation.com/iraq-war-20-years-on-how-the-world-failed-iraq-and-created-a-less-peaceful-democratic-and-prosperous-state-200075.

16. "Bombs away: John Bolton's most hawkish views on Iran, Iraq and North Korea," *The Guardian*, March 23, 2018, https://www.theguardian.com/us-news/2018/mar/23/john-bolton-north-korea-iran-iraq-who-is-he-what-does-he-believe.

17. "US Sanctions Caused Mass Civilian Deaths in Iraq. Afghan Civilians Are Up Next.," Truthout, February 8, 2022, https://truthout.org/articles/us-sanctions-caused-mass-civilian-deaths-in-iraq-afghan-civilians-are-up-next/.

18. John Bolton's prominence in the media proves our entire society is diseased," Monthly Review, March 22, 2023, https://mronline.org/2023/03/22/john-

boltons-prominence-in-the-media-proves-our-entire-society-is-diseased/.

19. "20 years after the Iraq invasion, John Bolton says he'd do it all over again," NPR, March 24, 2023, https://www.npr.org/2023/03/24/1165766356/20-years-after-the-iraq-invasion-john-bolton-says-hed-do-it-all-over-again.

20. "Bombs away: John Bolton's most hawkish views on Iran, Iraq and North Korea," *The Guardian*.

21. "Robert Gates Thinks Joe Biden Hasn't Stopped Being Wrong for 40 Years," *The Atlantic*, January 7, 2014, https://www.theatlantic.com/politics/archive/2014/01/robert-gates-thinks-joe-biden-hasnt-stopped-being-wrong-40-years/356785/.

22. "Biden Claims People Refer to Him as a 'Foreign Policy Expert'," TownHall.com, April 9, 2020, https://townhall.com/tipsheet/leahbarkoukis/2020/04/09/biden-foreign-policy-expert-n2566619.

23. "The Spies Who Came in to the TV Studio," Politico Magazine, February 6, 2018, https://www.politico.com/magazine/story/2018/02/06/john-brennan-james-claper-michael-hayden-former-cia-media-216943/.

24. "'Ministry of Truth' Trends on Twitter After Government Unveils New 'Disinformation Governance Board'," Foundation for Economic Education, April 28, 2022, https://fee.org/articles/ministry-of-truth-trends-on-twitter-after-government-unveils-new-disinformation-governance-board/.

25. "How the Biden Administration Caved to Republicans on Fighting Election Disinformation," ProPublica, November 1, 2022, https://www.pro-

publica.org/article/dhs-disinformation-elections-biden-gop-midterms.

26. "Biden administration defends disinformation board from fierce GOP criticism," CNN, May 2, 2022, https://www.cnn.com/2022/05/02/politics/dhs-disinformation-board/index.html.

27. "Anyone bestowing upon themselves…," @ggreenwald, Twitter, May 4, 2023, https://twitter.com/ggreenwald/status/1654521472814047237.

28. "What is a 'disinformation expert'?," @ggreenwald, Twitter, May 4, 2022, https://twitter.com/ggreenwald/status/1521906703293460480?s=20.

29. "White House's botched 'op'," *The New York Post*, October 6, 2009, https://nypost.com/2009/10/06/white-houses-botched-op/#comments.

30. Ibid.

31. Ibid.

32. Ibid.

33. "Americans' Trust in Scientists, Other Groups Declines," Pew Research Center, February 15, 2022, https://www.pewresearch.org/science/2022/02/15/americans-trust-in-scientists-other-groups-declines/.

34. "Amazon's latest health hire is a high-profile public health expert and 'lung doc'," CNBC, January 8, 2020, https://www.cnbc.com/2020/01/08/amazon-hires-vin-gupta-pulmonary-doctor-and-public-health-expert.html.

35. "A Popular Doctor Went On MSNBC To Advocate For Denying Anti-Vaxxers Access To Major Medical Treatments," Uproot, August 17, 2021, https://uproxx.com/viral/doctor-advocates-denying-anti-vaxxers-major-medical-treatments/.

36. "Covid fanatic & climate expert @VinGup-

taMD…," @tomselliott, Twitter, May 18, 2023, https://twitter.com/tomselliott/status/1659217374200094721.

37. "'60 Minutes' uses failed doomsday biologist to predict 'mass extinction' of humanity," Fox News, January 3, 2023, https://www.foxnews.com/media/60-minutes-uses-failed-doomsday-biologist-predict-mass-extinction-humanity.

38. Paul Ehrlich, *The Population Bomb* (Ballantine Books, 1971).

39. Ibid.

40. Paul Ehrlich, "Looking Backward From 2000 A.D.," *The Progressive*, April 1970, 23-25.

41. "You oughta make the FCC…," @AlexEpstein, Twitter, January 4, 2023, https://twitter.com/AlexEpstein/status/1610682756945825794.

42. Paul Ehrlich, quoted in Julian Simon, *The Ultimate Resource 2*, (Princeton: Princeton University Press, 1996), 35.

43. "Still Wrong! New Year's Paul Ehrlich Interview on CBS's 60 Minutes," Human Progress, January 2, 2023, https://www.humanprogress.org/still-wrong-new-years-paul-ehrlich-interview-on-cbss-60-minutes/.

44. "COVID vaccines: time to confront anti-vax aggression," Nature, April 27, 2021, https://www.nature.com/articles/d41586-021-01084-x.

45. "This Rogan/RFK/Hotez debate is wild…" @MitchellLandon, Twitter, June 18, 2023, https://twitter.com/MitchellLandon/status/1670546255343149062.

46. "Anti-Vaxxers Don't Want a Debate; They Want a Spectacle," *New York Magazine*, June 24, 2023, https://nymag.com/intelligencer/2023/06/robert-

f-kennedy-jr-vs-peter-hotez-would-not-be-a-debate.html.

47. "60 Minutes Promotes Paul Ehrlich's Failed Doomsaying One More Time," *Reason*, January 3, 2023, https://reason.com/2023/01/03/60-minutes-promotes-paul-ehrlichs-failed-doomsaying-one-more-time/.

48. "On CBS "60 Minutes…" @shellenberger, Twitter, January 3, 2023, https://twitter.com/shellenberger/status/1610357879076425728.

49. "60 Minutes extinction story…" @PaulREhrlich, Twitter, January 3, 2013, https://twitter.com/Paul-REhrlich/status/1610323659188486145; italics added.

50. "More than 99.9% of studies agree: Humans caused climate change," Phys.org, October 19, 2021, https://phys.org/news/2021-10-humans-climate.html.

51. "What Was Bloodletting All About?," Healthline, May 3, 2021, https://www.healthline.com/health/bloodletting.

52. "Cigarettes were once 'physician' tested, approved," Heal, March 10, 2009, https://www.healio.com/news/hematology-oncology/20120325/cigarettes-were-once-physician-tested-approved.

53. J.A. Bargh, M. Chen, and L. Burrows, "Automaticity of social behavior: Direct effects of trait construct and stereotype activation on action," Journal of Personality and Social Psychology, 71(2), 230–244.

54. Ibid.

55. Ibid.

56. Daniel Kahneman, *Thinking Fast and Slow* (New York: Farrar, Straus and Giroux, 2011), 57.

57. "The Hot and Cold of Priming," Science News, May 4, 2012, https://www.sciencenews.org/article/hot-and-cold-priming.

58. "Psychology's Replication Crisis Is Running Out of Excuses," *The Atlantic*, November 19, 2018, https://www.theatlantic.com/science/archive/2018/11/psychologys-replication-crisis-real/576223/.

59. "Interesting results: Can they be replicated?," American Psychological Association, February 2013, https://www.apa.org/monitor/2013/02/results.

60. "Experimental Economics Replication Project," accessed August 13, 2023, https://experimental-econreplications.com/.

61. "Larger sample sizes needed to increase reproducibility in neuroscience studies," ScienceDaily, June 7, 2018, https://www.sciencedaily.com/releases/2018/06/180607082544.htm.

62. "Replicating research in ecology and evolution: feasibility, incentives, and the cost-benefit conundrum," BMC Biology, October 28, 2015, https://bmcbiol.biomedcentral.com/articles/10.1186/s12915-015-0196-3.

63. "Replication studies in economics—How many and which papers are chosen for replication, and why?," *Research Policy*, vol. 48, issue 1, February 2019, 62-83.

64. "Replications in Psychology Research: How Often Do They Really Occur?," PubMed, November 2012, https://pubmed.ncbi.nlm.nih.gov/26168110/.

65. "Your brain on the scientific method," Oxford University Press, May 17, 2016, https://blog.oup.com/2016/05/brain-scientific-method/.

66. "Super Bowls: Serving Bowl Size and Food Consumption," Journal of the American Medical Association, April 13, 2005, https://jamanetwork. com/journals/jama/fullarticle/200673.

67. "New Study Finds Eggs Will Break Your Heart," Physicians Committee for Responsible Medicine, March 16, 2019, https://www.pcrm.org/news/ blog/new-study-finds-eggs-will-break-your-heart.

68. "Associations of Dietary Cholesterol or Egg Consumption With Incident Cardiovascular Disease and Mortality," *Journal of the American Medical Association*, March 19, 2019, https://jamanetwork. com/journals/jama/article-abstract/2728487.

69. Matthew Walker, *Why We Sleep* (London: Allen Lane, 2017), 3-4.

70. "Cornell Food Researcher's Downfall Raises Larger Questions For Science," NPR, September 26, 2018, https://www.npr.org/sections/the-salt/2018/09/26/651849441/cornell-food-research-ers-downfall-raises-larger-questions-for-science.

71. "Revisiting Eggs and Dietary Cholesterol," Less Likely, March 22, 2019, https://web.archive.org/ web/20190326094902/https://lesslikely.com/nutri-tion/eggs-cholesterol/.

72. Ibid.

73. "Matthew Walker's "Why We Sleep" Is Riddled with Scientific and Factual Errors," Alex Gauzy, November 15, 2019, https://guzey.com/books/ why-we-sleep/#also-no----sleeping-less-than-6-hours-a-night-does-not-double-your-risk-of-cancer.

74. Stuart Ritchie, *Science Fictions: How Fraud, Bias, Negligence, and Hype Undermine the Search for Truth* (New York: Metropolitan Books, 2020), 7.

75. "3M Survey: More Americans Trust Science," *Mpls.St.Paul Magazine*, January 3, 2023, https://mspmag.com/arts-and-culture/3m-survey-science-trust/.

BRAIN PAIN

1. "History of the Central Intelligence Agency," Wikipedia, accessed August 23, 2023, https://en.wikipedia.org/wiki/History_of_the_Central_Intelligence_Agency.
2. Ibid.
3. "Summary of Remarks by Mr. Allen W. Dulles at the National Alumni Conference of the Graduate Council of Princeton University," Central Intelligence Agency, accessed August 23, 2023, https://www.cia.gov/readingroom/document/cia-rdp70-00058r000200050069-9.
4. Ibid.
5. Ibid.
6. "Project MKULTRA, the CIA's Program of Research in Behavioral Modification," Joint Hearing Before the Select Committee on Intelligence and the Subcommittee on Health and Scientific Research of the Committee on Human Resources, August 3, 1977, https://www.google.com/books/edition/Project_MKULTRA_the_CIA_s_Program_of_Res/TEqhqtrF3XEC.
7. Edward Bernays, "The Engineering of Consent," *The Annals of the American Academy.*
8. Bernays, *Propaganda*, 38.
9. "Teen loses $25,000 after falling for phone scam," *The New York Post*, January 7, 2023, https://nypost.

com/2023/01/07/teen-loses-25000-after-falling-for-phone-scam/.

10. Ibid.

11. "Internet Crime Report 2021," Federal Bureau of Investigation, https://www.ic3.gov/Media/PDF/AnnualReport/2021_IC3Report.pdf, 19.

12. "The perfect job? Dream on! Five signs a job offer is a scam," We Live Security, April 25, 2014, https://www.welivesecurity.com/2014/04/25/the-perfect-job-dream-on-five-signs-a-job-offer-is-a-scam/.

13. "A new trend is causing teens to be vulnerable to human trafficking," Fox29, January 18, 2021, https://www.fox29.com/news/a-new-trend-is-causing-teens-to-be-vulnerable-to-human-trafficking.

14. "'Sextortion' predators target 14- to 17-year-old boys in new online scam," *The New York Post*, July 22, 2022, https://nypost.com/2022/07/22/new-sextortion-scheme-targets-14-to-17-year-old-boys/.

15. "Teens are eating laundry detergent for the 'Tide Pod Challenge,'" CBS News, January 12, 2018, https://www.cbsnews.com/news/tide-pod-challenge-ingesting-detergent-risks/.

16. Why Are Teen Brains Designed for Risk-taking?," Psychology Today, June 9, 2015, https://www.psychologytoday.com/us/blog/the-wide-wide-world-psychology/201506/why-are-teen-brains-designed-risk-taking.

17. "The Teenage Brain: Peer Influences on Adolescent Decision Making," *Current Directions in Psychological Science*, vol. 22, no. 2, April 2013, 114-120.

18. "Why Are Teen Brains Designed for Risk-taking?"

19. Ibid.
20. "Understanding the Teen Brain," Stanford Medicine Children's Health, accessed August 24, 2023, https://www.stanfordchildrens.org/en/topic/default?id=understanding-the-teen-brain-1-3051.
21. "What neuroscience tells us about the teenage brain," American Psychological Association, July 1, 2022, https://www.apa.org/monitor/2022/07/feature-neuroscience-teen-brain.
22. William L. Shirer, *Rise And Fall Of The Third Reich: A History of Nazi Germany* (New York: Simon & Schuster, 1990), 249.
23. Ibid.
24. Barbara Demick, *Nothing to Envy: Ordinary Lives in North Korea* (New York: Random House, 2009), 47.
25. Vladimir Lenin, from his speech at the First All-Russian Educational Congress, August 28, 1918, *Collected Works Volume XXIII* (1918-1919), 215.
26. Mary Tyler Peabody Mann, *The Life of Horace Mann* (Boston: Walker, Fuller & Company, 1865), 83.
27. Horace Mann, *Lectures and Annual Reports of Education* (Cambridge, 1867), 210.
28. Adolf Hitler, *Mein Kampf*, Project Gutenberg edition, https://gutenberg.net.au/ebooks02/0200601.txt.
29. Milton Mayer, *They Thought They Were Free: The Germans, 1933-45* (Chicago: The University of Chicago Press, 1955), xix.
30. Ibid.
31. Ibid., 166-67.
32. Thomas Blass, "The Man Who Shocked The World," Psychology Today, March 2002, https://

www.psychologytoday.com/intl/articles/200203/
the-man-who-shocked-the-world.

33. "How Much Energy Does the Brain Use?,"
Brain Facts.org, February 1, 2019, https://www.
brainfacts.org/brain-anatomy-and-function/
anatomy/2019/how-much-energy-does-the-brain-
use-020119.

34. Daniel Goleman, *Emotional Intelligence: Why It
Can Matter More Than IQ* (New York: Bantam
Books, 2005), 17.

35. "David Copperfield - Vanishing the Statue of Liberty," YouTube, accessed October 3, 2023, https://
www.youtube.com/watch?v=823GNH4Rczg.

36. Nevil Maskelyne, *Our Magic: The Art and Theory
in Magic* (Chris Bianchi, 2013), 93.

37. "The Con of Propaganda," Psychology Today,
February 15, 2017, https://www.psychologytoday.
com/us/blog/insight-therapy/201702/the-con-
propaganda.

38. Stephen Law, *The War for Children's Minds* (New
York: Routledge, 2006), 53-4.

WIN THE WAR

1. *Abraham Lincoln: Speeches and Writings, 1859-
1865* (New York City: The Library of America,
1989), 358.

2. Ibid., 32.

3. For more on Lincoln, see Thomas DiLorenzo,
The Real Lincoln (New York City: Crown Forum,
2003).

4. Alex Epstein, "25 Myths," Energy Talking Points,
accessed October 6, 2023, https://energytalking-
points.com/25-myths/.

5. Ibid.

6. J. Samuel Walker, "History, Collective Memory, and the Decision to Use the Bomb," *Diplomatic History 19, no. 2* (Spring 1995): 320, 323–25.

7. Thomas Powers, "Was It Right?," *The Atlantic*, July 1995, https://www.theatlantic.com/magazine/archive/1995/07/was-it-right/376364/.

8. Gar Alperovitz, *The Decision to Use the Atomic Bomb* (New York: Vintage Books, 1996), 355.

9. D. Michael Quinn, *Elder Statesman: A Biography of J. Reuben Clark* (Salt Lake City: Signature Books, 2002), 306.

10. "August Landmesser, shipyard worker in Hamburg, refused to perform Nazi salute (photo)," *The Washington Post*, February 7, 2012, https://www.washingtonpost.com/blogs/blogpost/post/august-landmesser-shipyard-worker-in-hamburg-refused-to-perform-nazi-salute-photo/2012/02/07/gIQA1ZzExQ_blog.html.

11. "Tank Man," Wikipedia, accessed October 7, 2023, https://en.wikipedia.org/wiki/Tank_Man.

12. "Meet 12yo Jaiden…," @cboyack, Twitter, August 29, 2023, https://twitter.com/cboyack/status/1696508336345153691.

13. Jaiden's mother secretly recorded video of the conversation with the vice principal. After local media declined to cover the story, she sent me the video asking for help. I shared it the following morning, where within 48 hours it had tens of millions of views.

14. "August Landmesser," Wikipedia, accessed October 7, 2023, https://en.wikipedia.org/wiki/August_Landmesser.

15. "World marks 30 years since Tiananmen massacre

as China censors all mention," CNN, June 4, 2019, https://www.cnn.com/2019/06/03/asia/tiananmen-june-4-china-censorship-intl/index.html.

16. "Aleksandr Solzhenitsyn," Wikipedia, accessed October 7, 2023, https://en.wikipedia.org/wiki/Aleksandr_Solzhenitsyn.

17. Aleksandr Solzhenitsyn, "Live Not By Lies," The Aleksandr Solzhenitsyn Center, accessed October 7, 2023, https://www.solzhenitsyncenter.org/live-not-by-lies.

18. "Planned Parenthood doctor tells committee that 'men can have pregnancies, especially trans men,'" The Washington Times, September 29, 2022, https://www.washingtontimes.com/news/2022/sep/29/planned-parenthood-doctor-tells-committee-men-can-/.

19. "Understanding the Proper Meaning of "Equality,'" Mises Institute, October 29, 2020, https://mises.org/wire/understanding-proper-meaning-equality.

20. "The Medical Community Says Abortion Access Is Health Care. Here's Why," CNET, June 24, 2022, https://www.cnet.com/health/medical/the-medical-community-says-abortion-access-is-health-care-heres-why/.

21. "In 2020, Words Are 'Violence,' Arson Is Not," Reason, July 3, 2020, https://reason.com/2020/07/03/silence-is-violence-george-floyd-protests-arson-is-not/.

22. "The CDC (Finally) Admitted the Science on Natural Immunity. Why Did It Take so Long?," Foundation for Economic Education, August 22, 2022, https://fee.org/articles/the-cdc-finally-admitted-the-science-on-natural-immunity-why-did-it-take-so-long/.

23. "Math professor claims equation 2+2=4 'reeks of white supremacist patriarchy," *The Washington Examiner*, August 10, 2010, https://www.washingtonexaminer.com/news/math-professor-claims-equation-2-2-4-reeks-of-white-supremacist-patriarchy.

24. George Orwell, *1984* (New York: Signet Classics, 1949), 250-251.

25. Ibid., 80-81.

26. Inge Jens, ed., *At the Heart of the White Rose: Letters and Diaries of Hans and Sophie Scholl* (New York: Plough Publishing House, 2017), 227.

27. Ibid.

28. Kathryn J. Atwood, *Women Heroes of World War II: 26 Stories of Espionage, Sabotage, Resistance, and Rescue* (Chicago: Chicago Review Press, 2011), 15.

29. Ibid.

30. "Leaflet 2," Center for White Rose Studies, accessed October 8, 2023, https://www.white-rose-studies.org/pages/leaflet-2.

31. Ibid.

32. "Leaflet 5," Center for White Rose Studies, accessed October 8, 2023, https://www.white-rose-studies.org/pages/leaflet-5.

33. "Leaflet 6," Center for White Rose Studies, accessed October 8, 2023, https://www.white-rose-studies.org/pages/leaflet-6.

34. Solzhenitsyn, "Live Not By Lies."

35. "Sophie Scholl," Spartacus Educational, accessed October 8, 2023, https://spartacus-educational.com/GERschollS.htm.

36. George H. Smith, "John Locke: In Search of the Radical Locke," Libertarianism.org, December 4,

2015, https://www.libertarianism.org/columns/
john-locke-search-radical-locke.

37. John Locke, *Second Treatise of Government*, Project Gutenberg, accessed October 8, 2023, https://www.gutenberg.org/files/7370/7370-h/7370-h.htm.

38. "United States Declaration of Independence," Wikipedia, accessed October 15, 2023, https://en.wikipedia.org/wiki/United_States_Declaration_of_Independence#Publication_and_reaction.

39. Pauline Maier, *American Scripture: Making the Declaration of Independence* (New York: Knopf, 1997), 156.

40. "On This Day in History - July 9, 1776," Revolutionary War and Beyond, accessed October 15, 2023, https://www.revolutionary-war-and-beyond.com/declaration-of-independence-read-troops-new-york-city.html.

41. Sasquatch music festival 2009 - Guy starts dance party," YouTube, accessed October 15, 2023, https://www.youtube.com/watch?v=GA8z7f7a2Pk.

CONCLUSION

1. "Sun Tzu's Art of War," Sonshi, accessed October 19, 2023, https://www.sonshi.com/sun-tzu-art-of-war-translation-original.html; emphasis added.
2. Ibid.

ABOUT THE AUTHOR

Connor Boyack is founder and president of Libertas Institute, an award-winning, multi-state solutions lab.

Named one of Utah's most politically influential people by *The Salt Lake Tribune*, Connor's leadership has led to changing over 100 laws covering a wide range of areas such as privacy, government transparency, property rights, drug policy, education, personal freedom, and more.

A public speaker and author of over 40 books which have sold over 5 million copies, Connor is best known for The Tuttle Twins children's book series which introduces young readers to the ideas of a free society.

Connor lives near Salt Lake City, Utah, with his wife and two children.

Find Boyack's books for sale at Libertas.org/shop/

Folk Medicine
Jarvis